MODERN
woman
MAGAZINE

FAMILY
FAVOURITES
FOR
EVERY DAY

MODERN
woman
MAGAZINE

FAMILY
FAVOURITES
FOR
EVERY DAY

MEALS MADE EASY

Macmillan Canada

Canadian Cataloguing in Publication Data

Main entry under title:

Modern woman cookbook: family favourites for every day

Includes index.

ISBN 0-7715-7618-8

1. quick and easy cookery.

TX833.5.M62 1998   641.5'55   C98-930951-7

This book is available at special discounts for bulk purchases by your group or organization for sales promotions, premiums, fundraising and seminars. For details, contact: Macmillan Canada, Special Sales Department, 29 Birch Avenue, Toronto, ON M4V 1E2. Tel: 416-963-8830

Cover photograph:

    Art Direction–Kim Woodside

    Photography–Shun Sasabuchi

    Food Styling–Nanci Clesse

    Prop Styling–Natalie Ogura

Interior photography: *Modern Woman* staff photographers

Modern Woman recipes developed by Heather Trim, Food Editor

Copyediting (recipes):Suzanne Moutis

Text design and typesetting: Tania Craan

We acknowledge the financial support of the Government of Canada through the Book Publishing Industry Development Program for our publishing activities.

Macmillan Canada

CDG Books Canada Inc.

Toronto, Ontario, Canada

1   2   3   4   5   TRI   03   02   01   00   99

Printed in Canada

A special thank you to everyone involved in producing our first *Modern Woman* cookbook. First to Heather Trim, for initially developing and testing the recipes; Lee Simpson, for her continuing support; Karen O'Reilly, our agent, who guided us through the process, and Judy Allen, who adds her special touch to each issue of *Modern Woman* and particularly to this cookbook. Thanks also to Macmillan Canada, for their patience in contract negotiations; Jill Lambert, for her superb advice, and to all the *Modern Woman* staff who provide their enthusiasm in producing each issue of *Modern Woman* magazine. Lastly, a heartfelt thanks to our loyal readers, who, by providing their cherished recipes, play a large part in making this cookbook unique.

Vivian Ip
Project Manager

CONTENTS

Magic with Leftovers

Celebrity Burgers

No Fuss Desserts

THE GREAT CANADIAN COOKIE SWAP

COOKBOOK INTRODUCTION

If you're like me, from Monday to Friday, 52 weeks a year, you hear voices — big and small — asking, "What's for dinner?"

It makes no difference whether the question's posed by the under-four-foot crowd or the bigger variety of kid, we all know what it means. Time to get dinner on the table — fast!

That's why we've created *FAMILY FAVOURITES FOR EVERY DAY* — this special cookbook of nearly 200 *Modern Woman* recipes for weekday meals.

Whether your after-five routine involves feeding the kids before ferrying them to arenas, music classes and swimming lessons, or a let's-eat-together family meal, one thing's for sure: we don't have a lot of time to spend shopping for or cooking complicated food. So we've included recipes that call for ingredients you're likely to have in your kitchen cupboard or fridge. And then we go a step further and include more timesaving options:

- *MW* Tips help you cut down on preparation time

- *MW* Cheats suggest substitutions when you might not have an ingredient on hand

- QUICK & EASY tells you a recipe is really speedy to make, like our Quick Chili Lasagna

- ONE POT dinners let you cut down on cleanup time

But there's more to feeding a family than oven-to-table time. You want to be sure they're eating nutritious, good-for-them food. So we've included nutrient information and we tell you when you'll get a bonus nutrition boost:

power PICK • POWER PICK lets you know whether a recipe is high in fibre, protein or vitamins

weight SMART • WEIGHT SMART recipes aren't loaded with fat or calories. They're all healthy choices with great taste.

We've even included photographs of some of our favourite recipes to whet your appetite.

And if you've ever wondered how the rich and famous dine, guess what? It's burgers for supper just like the rest of us. So eat like a star and sample Céline Dion's '50s burger from Nickels in Montreal, or Elvis Stojko's favourite, created he says "by my mother, and it's the very best I've ever tasted."

What's the real test for a recipe? Your family begs for more. Time after time. So we've included dozens of recipes from *Modern Woman* readers. People just like you — Canadians from every culture, who count on tried-and-true meals to satisfy their family's suppertime feeding frenzy with healthy, great-tasting food.

We hope you'll share your family's favourite meal with the rest of us. Write us today, and your recipe could be published in *Modern Woman* — the magazine, or our next cookbook.

Good eating! That's what *Modern Woman* recipes are all about.

Judy Allen
Editor, **MODERN** *woman*

SOUPS AND SALADS

During the hectic work and school week, it seems next to impossible to find time to add a first course to the family's meal. This chapter is full of ideas for easy soups and simple nutritious salads. Who says you can't have a soup and salad dinner? There's nothing like warm, satisfying soup, and bright, festive salads as a sure way to encourage your whole family to eat some vitamin-rich vegetables.

Whether it's Spinach Salad or Crunchy Coleslaw, the salads in this chapter are as good to eat as they are good for you. The soups — such as Hearty Lentil and Buffy Sainte-Marie's Corn Chowder — are chock-full of flavor and the kind of homemade goodness we all want to provide for our families every day.

SPICY CARROT SOUP

Carrot soup is a terrific way to get kids to eat their vegetables.

Serves 6

1 tbsp	vegetable oil
2	leeks, well washed and chopped, or 1 chopped onion
2	garlic cloves, minced
1 tbsp	finely chopped ginger
1 ½ tsp	ground cumin
½ tsp	medium curry powder
4 cups	sliced carrots (about 1 lb)
4 cups	chicken stock
½ cup	orange juice
¼ tsp	cayenne
	Salt and freshly ground black pepper
	Yogurt or sour cream

1. Heat oil in a large saucepan over medium heat. Add leeks, garlic, ginger, cumin and curry powder. Cook, stirring frequently, for about 2 minutes, until leeks have softened slightly.
2. Add carrots, chicken stock, orange juice and cayenne. Bring to a boil, reduce heat and simmer, uncovered, for 20 to 25 minutes or until carrots are very tender.
3. Using a food processor, process until soup is very smooth. Return to saucepan, and stir in salt and pepper to taste. Serve hot and top with a dollop of yogurt or sour cream.

Per portion: 101 calories, 4.7 g protein, 3.5 g fat, 13.2 g carbohydrates, 2.5 g dietary fibre, 43 mg calcium, 1.3 mg iron

To wash dirt from leeks, cut off and discard the green part (or save it for stock). Horizontally slice the white part of the leek through to the base, leaving the base intact. Rinse the inside of the leek under cold running water.

HEARTY LENTIL SOUP

 Lentils are a natural health food — they're chock-full of protein, carbohydrates, iron and B vitamins.

Makes 10 cups

1 tbsp	olive oil
1	onion, diced
2	garlic cloves, minced
1	carrot, chopped
1 stalk	celery, chopped
1	red pepper, seeded and chopped
2 tbsp	lemon juice
1 tsp	ground cumin
½ tsp	cinnamon
¼ tsp	cayenne
1	28-oz can plum tomatoes, including juice
4 cups	chicken or vegetable broth
1 cup	dry lentils
½ tsp	salt
1	potato, cut into ½-inch chunks

1. Heat oil in a large saucepan over medium heat. Add onion, garlic, carrot and celery and cook for 3 to 5 minutes, stirring occasionally, until the onion has softened slightly. Add red pepper, lemon juice and spices and cook for 2 minutes. Add tomatoes, chicken broth, lentils and salt, and bring liquid to a boil. Use the back of a spoon to crush tomatoes slightly while waiting for the liquid to boil.
2. Cover, reduce heat and simmer gently for 25 minutes. Add potato, cover and simmer for 10 to 15 minutes until lentils and potatoes are tender.

Per cup: 134 calories, 8.4 g protein, 2.5 g fat, 20.9 g carbohydrates,
4.2 g dietary fibre, 49 mg calcium, 2.9 mg iron

 Lentils are one of the few dried beans that do not need to be soaked. All beans should be rinsed and picked over to remove any small stones.

STICK-TO-YOUR-RIBS CHICKEN AND CHILI SOUP

Serve this hearty soup with thick bread and cheese for a light dinner.

Makes 8 cups

2 tbsp	vegetable oil
1 large	onion, chopped
4	garlic cloves, minced
1	green pepper, chopped
1	jalapeño pepper, finely minced
1	28-oz can whole plum tomatoes
2 cups	chicken broth
1	19-oz can black beans or kidney beans, drained and rinsed
½ tsp	Tabasco
2 cups	shredded cooked chicken or turkey
2 tbsp	lime juice
½ cup	finely chopped coriander
	Toppings: grated cheddar cheese, green onion and sour cream (optional)

1. Heat oil in a large saucepan over medium heat. Add onion, garlic, green pepper and jalapeño pepper. Cook, stirring frequently, until onion is soft, about 5 minutes. Stir in tomatoes, chicken broth, beans and Tabasco. Use the back of a spoon to crush tomatoes into bite-sized pieces. Bring mixture to a boil, cover, reduce heat and simmer for 15 minutes to allow flavors to blend.
2. Stir in chicken, lime juice and coriander. Taste and add salt and pepper if necessary. Top with your favourite toppings.

Per serving: 205 calories, 18.5 g protein, 7.4 g fat, 16.4 g carbohydrates, 5.4 g dietary fibre, 46 mg calcium, 1.8 mg iron. High in dietary fibre. Good source of vitamin C.

Instead of cooking chicken for this recipe, buy a cooked roasted chicken from the deli section of your supermarket, or use leftovers.

SOUTHBROOK CIDER SQUASH SOUP

Southbrook Farms, located just outside of Toronto, is a great place for a family outing. Family fun includes pick-your-own fields of seasonal fruits and vegetables, or you can buy home-grown produce if you don't feel like doing the picking.

Serves 6

2 medium	squash such as acorn, butternut or buttercup
1 tbsp	butter
1 medium	onion, chopped
1 tbsp	curry powder
1 ½ cups	chicken stock
1 ½ to 2 cups	cider or apple juice
2 medium	potatoes, diced
2	cobs of corn, kernels removed
¾ cup	yogurt or sour cream
	Garnish: peach or mango chutney, yogurt or sour cream

1. Preheat oven to 350F. Place squash on a cookie sheet and bake for 30 minutes. Remove one squash from the oven; peel squash, and remove seeds. Chop the flesh and set it aside. Leave the other squash to continue baking for another 30 minutes.

2. In a large saucepan, melt butter over medium heat. Add onion and cook for 3 minutes until soft. Add curry powder and stir and cook for 1 to 3 minutes. Remove second squash from oven and peel, seed and chop. Add this flesh to the onion mixture along with ¾ cup chicken stock. Cook, covered, for 10 minutes. Purée in food processor until smooth. Return mixture to the saucepan along with 1½ cups cider, potatoes, corn kernels and flesh from first squash. Cook, covered, for 10 minutes or until potatoes are tender. Stir in yogurt or sour cream. Heat, but do not boil. Add remaining cider if you would like a thinner soup. Garnish with a dollop of yogurt or sour cream and chutney.

Per portion: 175 calories, 4.9 g protein, 3 g fat, 35.9 g carbohydrates,
4.6 g dietary fibre, 86 mg calcium, 2 mg iron.

CAULIFLOWER AND CHEDDAR SOUP

power PICK This nutritious soup can be made ahead and reheated at a moment's notice.

Makes 6 cups

1 tbsp	vegetable or olive oil
1	onion, finely chopped
2 medium	carrots, thinly sliced
4 cups	cauliflower florets, about ½ a small head of cauliflower
4 cups	chicken broth
½ tsp	mustard powder
2 cups	grated old cheddar cheese
	Salt and pepper to taste

1. Heat oil in a large saucepan over medium heat. Add onion and carrots and cook, stirring frequently, until onion is soft, about 5 minutes. Add cauliflower florets, chicken broth and mustard powder to the saucepan. Bring to a boil, reduce heat and simmer, covered, for 15 to 20 minutes, until cauliflower is very tender.

2. Transfer to a food processor or blender and purée until smooth, scraping down sides if necessary. Return soup to low heat. Stir in cheese until melted. Add salt and pepper to taste.

Per serving: 232 calories, 14.4 g protein, 15.9 fat, 8.3 g carbohydrates, 2.1 g dietary fibre, 308 mg calcium, 1.1 mg iron. Moderate in dietary fibre. Excellent source of vitamin C and calcium.

SPICY WINTER VEGETABLE SOUP

Here's a great way to put some spice into a cold winter's day.

Makes 6 cups

1 tbsp	vegetable oil
1	onion, chopped
1 small	jalapeño pepper, seeded (optional)
1 tbsp	curry powder or garam masala
1 small	rutabaga, peeled and chopped (about 4 cups)
2 medium	carrots, sliced
4 cups	chicken broth
1	pear, peeled and cored
	Salt and pepper to taste

1. Heat oil in a large saucepan over medium heat. Add onion, jalapeño pepper and curry powder. Cook, stirring frequently, for about 2 minutes. Add rutabaga, carrots and chicken broth. Cover and bring to a boil. Reduce heat and simmer for about 30 minutes until vegetables are tender. Stir in pear and continue to simmer about 5 more minutes until pear is tender.

2. Purée soup in a food processor or blender until smooth. Add salt and pepper to taste. If soup is a little thick, thin with a little more chicken broth, cream or water.

Per cup: 112 calories, 5 g protein, 3.7 g fat, 15.9 g carbohydrates, 3.5 g dietary fibre, 63 mg calcium, 1.3 mg iron. Good source of vitamin C and contains a moderate amount of fibre.

The jalapeño pepper gives the soup a bit of heat but can be left out if you prefer. You can also substitute a pinch of cayenne pepper or chili flakes for the jalapeño.

BUFFY SAINTE-MARIE'S CORN CHOWDER

Buffy Sainte-Marie was inducted into the Juno Hall of Fame in 1996 for her long-standing contribution to Canadian music. This is her contribution to Canadian kitchens. Her rich-tasting soup is delicious even without the fish and is low in calories.

Serves 12

6 medium	potatoes, peeled and cut into chunks
3 tbsp	sesame oil
6	garlic cloves, minced
10	cobs of corn (kernels removed) or 4 (12–oz) drained cans of corn
1 lb	firm white fish, cut into bite-sized cubes (optional)
1 tbsp	vegetable or chicken bouillon powder
1	10-oz can cream of potato or chicken soup
2	cans evaporated milk
	Salt and pepper to taste

1. Bring a large pot of salted water to a boil. Add about 2 cups potato cubes, then 3 minutes later add remaining potatoes (the softer potatoes will help thicken the soup). When the large pieces seem nearly done, drain, reserving ½ cup liquid. Set potatoes aside. Rinse and dry saucepan.
2. Heat 1 tablespoon of sesame oil in the pot, add half the garlic and cook for 1 minute. Add corn and cook for 2 minutes. Add cooked potatoes, and mix gently. Remove from heat.
3. Heat remaining sesame oil over medium-high heat in a large frying pan. Add remaining garlic; cook for 1 minute. Add fish (if using) and stir until cooked. Add fish to potato-corn mixture. Stir bouillon into 2 tablespoons of hot water. Add to corn mixture along with potato soup, evaporated milk and reserved potato water. Cover and heat, but do not boil. Add salt and pepper to taste. For best flavor, refrigerate overnight, or for at least 1 hour, then reheat. Serve with sourdough bread.

Per serving: 309 calories, 9.7 g protein, 10.7 g fat, 48.4 g carbohydrates, 4.7 g dietary fibre, 192 mg calcium, 1 mg iron. Good source of calcium and high in dietary fibre.

If this recipe makes more than you can use at one time, freeze the leftovers.

CREAMY MUSHROOM SOUP

There's nothing like homemade soup to warm your family on a cold winter's night.

Makes 4 cups

2 tbsp	butter
1 cup	finely chopped green onions (about 6)
2	garlic cloves, minced
½ cup	dry white wine
1¼ lb	medium-sized mushrooms, chopped
1½ cups	chicken broth
¼ tsp	thyme
½ cup	half-and-half cream
2 tbsp	finely chopped parsley
	Salt and pepper to taste

1. Heat butter in a large saucepan over medium heat. Add green onions and garlic and cook, stirring occasionally, just until onions are soft. Increase heat to high, add wine and boil until wine is reduced by half. Add mushrooms and cook, stirring occasionally, for 5 minutes. Add broth and thyme. Bring to a boil, cover and simmer for 10 minutes.

2. Purée three-quarters of the mixture in a food processor or blender until smooth, leaving remainder of soup in the saucepan. Return purée to the mixture in the saucepan. Stir in cream and parsley; warm the soup, but do not let it boil. Taste and add salt and pepper if necessary.

Per serving: 148 calories, 5.6 g protein, 9.9 g fat, 9.5 g carbohydrates, 2.9 g dietary fibre, 71 mg calcium, 2.7 mg iron. Good source of iron. Moderate in fibre.

CAESAR SALAD

Try the *MW* version of this classic favourite.

Serves 8

3 tbsp	lemon juice (about 1 lemon)
2	garlic cloves, crushed
1 tsp	anchovy paste
1 tsp	Dijon mustard
1 tsp	Worcestershire sauce
	Dash of Tabasco
	Salt and black pepper
½ cup	olive oil
1	large head romaine lettuce, torn into bite-sized pieces
2 cups	homemade or purchased croutons
½ cup	Parmesan cheese

1. In a small bowl, whisk lemon juice with garlic, anchovy paste, Dijon, Worcestershire sauce, Tabasco, salt and pepper. Gradually whisk in oil. Dressing can be made several days in advance; simply cover and refrigerate.

2. Toss lettuce with dressing in a large salad bowl. Add croutons and Parmesan and toss again.

Per serving: 201 calories, 5.3 g protein, 16 g fat, 9.7 g carbohydrates, 1.4 g dietary fibre, 132 mg calcium, 1.4 mg iron. Good source of vitamins A and C.

Homemade croutons are easy to make and ideal for using up day-old French, Italian or egg bread. Cut bread into 1/2-inch cubes and toss in a medium-sized bowl with 1 tablespoon oil and a generous grinding of black pepper. Turn onto a cookie sheet and bake in a preheated 350F oven, stirring occasionally until lightly toasted — 13 to 15 minutes; cool. Croutons can be stored in an airtight container for several days.

WARM POTATO AND SAUSAGE SALAD

Serve one of our robust soups with this hearty salad for a satisfying dinner that's quick and easy.

Serves 4

1 ½ lb	small potatoes, unpeeled
2	hot Italian sausages
⅓ cup	diced celery
½ small	red onion, cut into julienne strips
1	garlic clove, minced
2 tbsp	olive oil
2 tbsp	white wine vinegar
2 tsp	Dijon mustard
½ tsp each	salt and black pepper

1. If you have only large potatoes, cut them into bite-sized chunks. Put them in a saucepan and cover with cold water. Bring to a boil, add some salt and cook for 10 to 15 minutes, or just until tender (do not overcook).
2. Meanwhile, cut sausages into slices ½ inch thick. Fry them in a medium-sized frying pan for 10 to 12 minutes, until cooked through. Use a slotted spoon to remove them to a plate; cover to keep warm. Drain all but 2 teaspoons of fat from pan. Add celery, onion and garlic and cook for 2 minutes, stirring frequently, until barely tender. Add oil to pan; whisk in vinegar, Dijon, salt and pepper. Heat until warm.
3. Drain potatoes and put them in a serving bowl along with sausages. Toss with warm dressing. Serve warm over lettuce if you wish.

Per serving: 290 calories, 9.3 g protein, 15.1 g fat, 30.6 g carbohydrates, 2.6 g dietary fibre, 29 mg calcium, 1.7 mg iron. Good source of vitamin C; moderate source of fibre.

ADRIATIC PASTA SALAD

Make this salad even easier by replacing home roasted peppers with those found in jars in your supermarket.

Serves 4

2 ½ cups	fusilli, penne or rotini
2 ½ tbsp	olive oil
1 large	tomato, chopped
½ cup	½-inch cubes pepperoni or pepperettes
½ cup	½-inch cubes mozzarella or crumbled feta cheese
½ cup	chopped roasted red peppers
¼ cup	pitted black olives
1 tbsp	capers (optional)
2 tbsp	finely chopped fresh basil or parsley
½ tsp	salt
	Generous grinding of black pepper

1. Put pasta in a large pot of boiling, salted water and cook until just tender. Drain and rinse under cold water to stop the cooking. Toss pasta with oil.
2. Add remaining ingredients and toss well. Taste and add more salt if necessary.

Per serving: 432 calories, 14.4 g protein, 15.1 g fat, 59.1 g carbohydrates, 3.9 g dietary fibre, 81 mg calcium, 1.6 mg iron. Good source of vitamin C. High in dietary fibre.

THREE-BEAN SALAD

Fresh basil gives this salad a fresh-from-the-garden taste.

Serves 6

2 tsp	salt
½ lb	green beans, trimmed and cut in half
½ lb	yellow beans, trimmed and cut in half
1	19-oz can chickpeas, rinsed and drained well
3 tbsp	finely chopped red onion
3 tbsp	olive oil
2 tbsp	lemon juice

1 tsp	finely grated lemon peel
	Salt and black pepper to taste
¼ cup	finely chopped fresh basil

1. Bring a large pot of water to a boil; add salt. Add green and yellow beans to water and boil for 1 minute. Drain water and rinse beans under cold running water. Pat them dry and place them in a large salad bowl along with chickpeas. Toss with red onion.
2. Whisk oil with lemon juice, lemon peel, salt and pepper. Toss with bean mixture. Then toss with fresh basil.

Per serving: 173 calories, 6.1 g protein, 8 g fat, 21.5 g carbohydrates, 4 g dietary fibre, 83 mg calcium, 2.2 mg iron. Good source of iron; high in dietary fibre.

 To prevent basil from turning black, stir into salad just before serving.

POTATO SALAD

This salad is great with anything you've barbecued — burgers, ribs, chicken pieces — but makes a tasty companion to roasted chicken or cold roast beef.

Serves 8

2 ½ lb	potatoes, peeled and cut into 1-inch chunks
2	hard-boiled eggs, peeled and coarsely chopped
2	green onions, thinly sliced
¼ cup	finely diced dill pickles
¼ cup	finely diced celery
⅓ cup	mayonnaise (light or regular)
3 tbsp	buttermilk
½ tsp each	salt and pepper

1. Put potatoes in a medium-sized saucepan and cover with cold salted water. Bring to a boil, reduce heat and simmer, covered, until potatoes are just tender — 10 to 15 minutes (do not overcook). Drain well and cool. Put potatoes in a medium serving bowl and toss with eggs, green onions, pickles and celery.
2. Whisk together mayonnaise, buttermilk, 1 tablespoon pickle liquid, salt and pepper. Toss with potatoes. Taste and add more salt and pepper if needed.

Per serving: 143 calories, 3.7 g protein, 4.4 g fat, 22.6 g carbohydrates, 1.7 g dietary fibre, 27 mg calcium, 0.6 mg iron.

GREEK SALAD

Feta cheese and black olives add the Greek character to this great salad.

Serves 8

½ cup	olive oil
3 tbsp	red wine vinegar
1 tsp	dried oregano
½ tsp	salt
1 head	iceberg or romaine lettuce, torn into pieces
1	tomato, cut into wedges
⅓ cup	chopped green or white onion
2	radishes, thinly sliced
1	green pepper, cut into thin strips
½ cup	thinly sliced cucumber
½ cup	crumbled feta cheese
½ cup	black olives

1. In a small bowl, whisk together oil, vinegar, oregano and salt. Dressing can be made several days in advance; simply cover and refrigerate. Toss remaining ingredients together in a large salad bowl, then toss with dressing. Serve immediately.

Per serving: 166 calories, 2.3 g protein, 15.9 g fat, 4.8 g carbohydrates, 1.6 g dietary fibre, 68 mg calcium, 1 mg iron. Good source of vitamin C.

Several countries, including Canada, produce feta cheese. Feta is traditionally made with goat's or sheep's milk, but today it is also made with cow's milk. When choosing, ask to try different samples of feta cheese, if possible, as the type of milk used will make quite a difference in the taste. Feta cheese is usually quite salty, but levels differ, depending on the producer. Creaminess, texture and price will also vary significantly from brand to brand.

ZESTY CHICKEN SALAD

You can't beat this salad for a meal-in-a-bowl.

Serves 3

⅓ cup	vegetable oil
1 tsp	finely grated lime peel
¼ cup	lime juice (about 2 limes)
2 tsp	granulated sugar
1 tsp	curry powder
½ tsp each	ground cumin, ground ginger and salt
¼ tsp	cayenne
	Black pepper to taste
2	boneless, skinless chicken breasts, cut into thin strips
1 bunch	spinach, stems removed, torn into bite-sized pieces
2 medium	carrots, grated
1	firm, unpeeled apple, cut into bite-sized pieces
2 tbsp	coarsely chopped pecans, toasted
2 tbsp	raisins

1. In a small bowl, whisk vegetable oil with lime peel and juice, sugar, curry powder, cumin, ginger, salt, cayenne and pepper. In another small bowl, toss chicken with 2 tablespoons of the marinade. Let stand for 20 minutes.
2. Meanwhile, toss spinach (you should have 8 to 10 loosely packed cups) with carrots and apple. Heat a small non-stick frying pan over medium-high heat. Add chicken and sauté 5 to 7 minutes, until cooked through. Use a slotted spoon to remove chicken from pan, leaving liquid in pan. Toss chicken with spinach. Add remaining dressing to pan; heat until warm, then toss with spinach. Sprinkle with pecans and raisins. Serve immediately.

Per serving: 458 calories, 24 g protein, 29.5 g fat, 29.6 g carbohydrates, 6.9 g dietary fibre, 192 mg calcium, 5.7 mg iron. Very high in dietary fibre and iron.

EASY ASPARAGUS SALAD

This is a wonderful way to dress up fresh asparagus.

Serves 3

1 lb	asparagus, cut diagonally into 2 ½-inch pieces
2 tbsp	olive oil
1 tbsp	lemon juice
½ tsp	grainy Dijon mustard
	Salt and pepper to taste
2 tbsp	finely chopped red pepper
	Grated Parmesan cheese

1. Cook asparagus in a saucepan of boiling salted water for 2 to 3 minutes until barely tender. Drain well.
2. Meanwhile, whisk olive oil with lemon juice, Dijon, salt and pepper in a small bowl until combined. As soon as asparagus is drained, arrange on a plate. Top with red pepper. Drizzle with dressing, then sprinkle grated Parmesan on top.

Per portion: 117 calories, 3.8 g protein, 9.6 g fat, 6.6 g carbohydrates, 2.5 g dietary fibre, 30 mg calcium, 0.1 mg iron

When buying asparagus, look for straight, crisp spears with tightly closed tips. To store asparagus, set the bunch upright in a jug with a small amount of water, or wrap ends in a damp paper towel and cover the entire bunch with plastic wrap. Refrigerated it should keep for 2 to 3 days.

FETA, MINT AND BULGUR SALAD

If your family has never tried bulgur, why not introduce a new food tonight?

Serves 6

1 cup	medium-grain bulgur
½ cup	crumbled feta cheese, about 2 oz
1 large	tomato, seeded and chopped into ½-inch pieces
2	green onions, thinly sliced
½ cup	chopped cucumber (¼-inch pieces)
2 tbsp	finely chopped mint, basil or parsley
2 tbsp	olive oil
1 ½ tbsp	red wine vinegar
¼ tsp each	salt and freshly ground black pepper

1.   Bring a large pot of water to a boil. Add salt, then bulgur (just as you would cook pasta). Boil for 12 to 15 minutes or just until bulgur is tender but not mushy. Drain very well and refrigerate until cool.

2.   Meanwhile, put feta, tomato, green onions, cucumber and mint in a medium-sized serving bowl. Gently toss. In a small bowl, whisk oil with vinegar, salt and pepper.

3.   Add cooled bulgur to feta mixture and toss gently. Then toss with olive oil mixture. Taste and add more salt and pepper if necessary. Refrigerate until ready to serve. Salad tastes better if served within a of couple hours of being made.

Per portion: 148 calories, 4.3 g protein, 6.4 g fat, 20.4 g carbohydrates, 4.9 g dietary fibre, 52 mg calcium, 1.3 mg iron

Bulgur is a type of cracked wheat. Its nutty flavor is ideal for salads, or it can be used in a stuffing or in place of rice. Bulgur can be found in some super-markets, health food stores and bulk food stores. It is quick to prepare and high in dietary fibre.

CRUNCHY CHICKPEA SALAD

This flavorful salad can be prepared a day in advance, then covered and refrigerated. If prepared in advance, taste just before serving. It may require a little more lemon juice and seasonings.

Serves 6

1	28-oz can chickpeas
2 medium	carrots, sliced
1 small	red pepper, seeded and chopped
1	green onion, finely chopped
3 tbsp	lemon juice
1 tbsp	olive oil
¼ tsp	Tabasco
1 tsp each	ground cumin and chili powder
½ tsp each	salt and freshly ground black pepper
2 tbsp each	finely chopped Italian parsley, currants and toasted almonds

1. Drain chickpeas. Rinse them under cold running water, then pat dry. Put in a serving bowl. Toss them with carrots, red pepper and green onion.
2. In a small bowl, whisk lemon juice with oil, Tabasco, cumin, chili powder, salt and pepper. Pour onto chickpea mixture and toss. Sprinkle with parsley, currants and almonds and toss again.

Per portion: 189 calories, 8 g protein, 5.4 g fat, 29.3 g carbohydrates, 4.6 g dietary fibre, 50 mg calcium, 7.8 mg iron.

SPINACH SALAD WITH BLUE-CHEESE DRESSING

power PICK This salad appeared in *MW* as a Classic Salad Made Low Fat. You won't believe how good it tastes and with only 1.5 g of fat per serving!

Serves 8

⅓ cup	1% plain yogurt
1 ½ tbsp	red wine vinegar
1 ½ tsp	liquid honey
½ tsp	Dijon mustard
	Salt and pepper to taste

1 large	bunch spinach, torn into bite-sized pieces (about 12 cups)
6 slices	red onion, separated into rings
¼ cup	blue cheese, finely crumbled

1. Stir together yogurt, vinegar, honey, Dijon, salt and pepper until blended. Put spinach leaves in a large bowl along with onion rings. Toss with just enough dressing to coat leaves. Sprinkle with blue cheese and toss again.

Per serving: 45 calories, 3.8 g protein, 1.5 g fat, 5.6 g carbohydrates, 2.3 g dietary fibre, 123 mg calcium, 2.3 mg iron, 167 mcg folacin. Excellent source of vitamin A. Good source of vitamin C and iron. Moderate dietary fibre.

COLORFUL CRUNCHY COLESLAW

This salad is as wonderful to look at as it is to eat.

Serves 8

2 cups	coarsely grated green cabbage
2 cups	coarsely grated red cabbage
2	carrots, coarsely grated
2	green onions, thinly sliced
1	unpeeled apple, cored and cut into ½-inch pieces
1	unpeeled pear, cored and cut into ½-inch pieces
⅓ cup	smooth unsweetened applesauce
⅓ cup	buttermilk
1 ½ tbsp	cider vinegar
1 ½ tsp	Dijon mustard
	Salt and pepper to taste

1. Toss cabbage, carrots, green onions, apple and pear pieces together until combined.
2. Whisk applesauce with buttermilk, vinegar, Dijon, salt and pepper to taste. Toss with vegetables.

Per serving: 51 calories, 1.2 g protein, 0.4 g fat, 12 g carbohydrates, 2.4 g dietary fibre, 42 mg calcium, 0.5 mg iron, 21 mcg folacin. Excellent source of vitamin A. Good source of vitamin C. Moderate dietary fibre.

SIMPLE SOBA NOODLE SALAD

How about a taste of the Orient tonight?

Serves 2 to 3

½ lb	dried soba noodles
3 tbsp	soy sauce
2 tbsp	mirin (sweet cooking rice wine)
2 tsp	sesame oil
1	garlic clove, crushed
2	green onions, thinly sliced
¼ cup	coarsely grated carrot

1. Cook soba noodles in a large pot of boiling water following package directions (for about 7 minutes) until just tender. Drain and rinse under cold running water, combing back and forth with fingers to remove starch. Drain again. Put noodles in a serving bowl.
2. In a separate bowl, prepare dressing: stir together soy sauce, mirin, sesame oil and garlic. Toss drained noodles with onions and carrot. Mix noodles with dressing; serve immediately.

Per serving: 313 calories, 14.1 g protein, 3.3 g fat, 59.5 g carbohydrates, 0.5 g dietary fibre, 25 mg calcium, 1.8 mg iron, 28 mcg folacin. Excellent source of vitamin A.

TOMATO AND GREEN BEAN SALAD

This recipe comes from editor Judy Allen.

Serves 8

1 ¾ lb	green beans (about 5 cups)
3 large	tomatoes
8	mushrooms
⅔ cup	olive oil
¼ cup	balsamic or red wine vinegar
¼ cup	toasted pine nuts or slivered almonds
	Salt and pepper to taste

1. Bring a large pot of water to a boil. Meanwhile, trim ends from beans. (If beans are really long, cut them in half.) Put beans in pot, bring back to a boil

and cook for 2 to 3 minutes until tender-crisp. Drain beans and rinse them immediately in cold running water. Set them aside to finish draining.

2. Cut tomatoes into wedges. Slice mushrooms thinly. Gently toss beans, tomato wedges and mushrooms with oil and vinegar. Then toss with pine nuts, salt and pepper. Serve immediately.

Per serving: 234 calories, 3.8 g protein, 21 g fat, 11.9 g carbohydrates, 3.3 g dietary fibre, 45 mg calcium, 2 mg iron. Moderate in dietary fibre.

Toast pine nuts or almonds by spreading them evenly in a small pan and placing in a 350F oven. Heat for 5 to 10 minutes, stirring frequently (watch carefully, as they burn easily), until golden.

AUTUMN CHICKEN SALAD IN A PITA

This terrific salad-in-a-pita makes a healthy back-to-school or workday lunch.

Serves 1 to 2

1 cup	leftover cooked diced chicken
½ cup	diced unpeeled apple
1	green onion, finely chopped
1 tbsp	chopped cashews or walnuts
2 tbsp	currants or raisins
¼ cup	plain yogurt
1 tsp	lemon juice
¼ tsp	curry powder
	Dash of Tabasco
	Salt to taste
1	carrot, coarsely grated
1	7-inch pita bread, halved
	Lettuce leaves

1. In a medium bowl, stir together cooked chicken, apple, green onion, cashews and currants. In a small bowl, stir yogurt with lemon juice, curry powder and Tabasco. Toss yogurt mixture with chicken mixture; taste and add salt. Gently toss in carrot.

2. Open up each pita half, line with lettuce leaves, then fill with chicken mixture.

Per portion: 324 calories, 26.3 g protein, 8.9 g fat, 35.2 g carbohydrates, 2.7 g dietary fibre, 112 mg calcium, 2.7 mg iron, 42 mcg folacin. Excellent source of vitamin A, vitamin B6 and zinc. Good source of vitamin B12 and iron. Moderate in dietary fibre.

BARBECUED VEGETABLE AND PENNE SALAD

This salad is a sure winner served with a summer barbecue.

Serves 8

½	450-g pkg penne, fusilli or rotini
1 each	red and green peppers, cut into 1-inch wedges
1 small	zucchini, cut horizontally into ¼-inch slices
10	mushrooms
2	green onions
¼	cup olive oil
	Salt and pepper
2 medium	tomatoes, cut into chunks
⅓ cup	coarsely chopped fresh basil or parsley
¼ cup	pitted black olives
2 to 4 tbsp	red wine vinegar
½ tsp	Tabasco

1.   Preheat barbecue to medium. Cook pasta according to package directions. Drain and rinse it under cold water to stop the cooking, then drain again. Put it in a large serving bowl. Meanwhile, put peppers, zucchini, mushrooms and onions in a large bowl. Toss with 1 tbsp oil and a generous amount of salt and pepper. Put vegetables in a grill basket or on a barbecue vegetable tray. Barbecue, turning occasionally until tender.
2.   Remove vegetables from barbecue and place on a cutting board. Cut peppers and zucchini into large bite-sized pieces. Slice mushrooms and thinly slice onions. Toss with pasta, tomatoes, basil and olives.
3.   Whisk together remaining oil, 2 tbsp vinegar, Tabasco and salt to taste. If serving immediately, toss salad with dressing. If not, cover and refrigerate salad and dressing separately; toss just before serving. Taste and add remaining vinegar and more salt and Tabasco if necessary.

Per serving: 192 calories, 4.6 g protein, 7.9 g fat, 29.5 g carbohydrates, 2.9 g dietary fibre, 22 mg calcium, 1.2 mg iron. Excellent source of vitamin C. Moderate dietary fibre.

SENSATIONAL SIDE DISHES

Potatoes are one food kids will eat — that's why this chapter has seven recipes for preparing the popular spud. Rice, beans and vegetables are also featured in this chapter on what to serve along with your main dish. These recipes are as versatile as they are delicious. Baked beans are at home beside a side of ribs or on a plate of eggs and the Apple Rice Side Dish will dress up chicken, pork or fish.

RANCHMAN'S BAKED BEANS

MW READER RECIPE: The Ranchman's in Calgary has been serving home-style cooking with true western hospitality for more than 20 years. The chef suggests bringing a cowboy-sized appetite to enjoy these baked beans with plenty of cold ones and a 20-ounce T-bone for a Stampede'n good time.

Makes 8 servings

1	28-oz can beans with pork
¾ cup	finely chopped white onion
¼ cup	molasses
1 tbsp	mustard
1 tsp	Worcestershire sauce
½ cup	barbecue sauce
1 small	apple, peeled, cored and finely chopped
2 strips	bacon

1.   Preheat oven to 325F. Mix all ingredients together (except bacon) and transfer to an 8-inch square baking dish. Lay bacon on top. Bake, uncovered, in the preheated oven for 1 hour.

Per serving: 196 calories, 6.6 g protein, 3.3 g fat, 33.1 g carbohydrates, 7.3 g dietary fibre, 81 mg calcium, 2.5 mg iron

EGGPLANT DIP

Eggplant is an appetizing source of calcium.

Makes 1 cup

1	unpeeled eggplant
1 tbsp	sesame tahini
2 tbsp	lemon juice
1 ½ tsp	finely chopped parsley
½ tsp	ground cumin
	Generous pinch of cayenne
	Generous pinches of salt and black pepper
	Fresh raw vegetables, crackers or pita wedges

1. Preheat broiler. Place whole eggplant on a baking sheet and pierce its skin in several places with a fork. Broil eggplant about 3 inches away from heat. Turn occasionally until eggplant is tender and skin is blistered all over, 15 to 20 minutes. Remove from heat.

2. When eggplant is cool enough to handle, cut off stem and use a spoon to scrape the peel off; discard peel. Put eggplant in a food processor or blender along with remaining ingredients except raw vegetables and crackers and purée until smooth, scraping down sides of bowl occasionally.

3. Turn the purée into a bowl and serve with raw vegetables, crackers or pita wedges. This dip will keep in the refrigerator for about a week.

Per serving: 40 calories, 1.2 g protein, 2.2 g fat, 5.1 g carbohydrates, 1.9 g dietary fibre, 13 mg calcium, 0.7 mg iron

 This dip may become firmer when refrigerated, so bring it back to room temperature before serving and, if necessary, thin with a bit of water or lemon juice.

BLACK OLIVE SPREAD

This savory topping can be used to dress up vegetables or croutons.

Makes 1 cup

1 ½ cups	pitted black olives
1 tbsp	drained capers
2 tsp	anchovy paste
1 large	garlic clove, chopped
1 tsp	Italian seasoning
2 tbsp	lemon juice
2 tbsp	olive oil
	Salt and freshly ground pepper to taste

1. Put olives, capers, anchovy paste, garlic, Italian seasoning and lemon juice in a food processor and purée. With the machine running, gradually add olive oil into mixture until combined. Add black pepper. Taste and add salt as necessary. Serve with crusty bread or toast.

Per serving: 17 calories, 0.3 g protein, 1.4 g fat, 1.1 g carbohydrates, 0.4 g dietary fibre, 14 mg calcium, 0.5 mg iron

CHUNKY SUMMER VEGETABLE SPREAD

This spread is a delicious topping for burgers.

Makes 5 cups

1 tbsp	olive oil
1	onion, chopped
4	garlic cloves, minced
1 medium	unpeeled eggplant, cut into ½-inch chunks
3 stalks	celery, thinly sliced
2 small	zucchini, cut into ½-inch chunks
1	28-oz can plum tomatoes, including juice
3 tbsp	red wine vinegar
2 tbsp	granulated sugar
¼ to ½ tsp	hot chili flakes
⅓ cup	chopped parsley
¼ cup	chopped black olives
2 tbsp	drained capers
	Salt and freshly ground black pepper to taste
	Crackers or thinly sliced bread

1.   Heat oil in a large wide frying pan over medium heat. Add onion and garlic and cook, stirring occasionally, until onion is soft.

2.   Add eggplant, celery, zucchini, tomatoes and juice, vinegar, sugar and ¼ teaspoon chili flakes (if you like your food spicier, add the other ¼ teaspoon). Use the back of a spoon to crush tomatoes. Bring mixture to a boil, then reduce heat and cook, covered, stirring occasionally, until vegetables are tender — about 15 minutes. Remove cover and continue to simmer, stirring occasionally, until vegetables are very soft and mixture is thick, about 30 minutes.

3.   Remove from heat and stir in parsley, olives and capers. Taste and add salt and pepper. Serve at room temperature with crackers and bread. This mixture will keep, covered and refrigerated, for about a week.

Per serving: 33 calories, 0.8 g protein, 1 g fat, 6.1 g carbohydrates,
1.4 g dietary fibre, 21 mg calcium, 0.5 mg iron

 TIPS This recipe makes a large quantity, but it can be cut in half. Use it while still hot as a pasta sauce.

SPICED BASMATI RICE

Here's a simple way to add a taste of Indian cooking to tonight's menu.

Serves 4

1 cup	basmati or long-grain white rice
1 tbsp	butter
¼ cup	finely chopped onion
1	garlic clove, minced
1-inch chunk	ginger, peeled and finely chopped
1	cinnamon stick
6	whole cloves
6	whole black peppercorns
4	cardamom pods
1 ¾ cups	water
½ tsp	salt

1. If using basmati rice, rinse it several times under cold running water. Put rice in a bowl and cover with cold water. Let stand for 30 minutes. Drain rice. If using long-grain white rice, do not rinse, soak or drain.
2. Melt butter over medium heat in a medium-sized saucepan. Add onion, garlic, ginger, cinnamon, cloves, peppercorns and cardamom. Cook for about 3 minutes or just until onion softens. Stir in rice. Add water (if using long-grain rice increase water by ¼ cup) and salt.
3. Bring to a boil. Cover, reduce heat to low and cook for 10 minutes for basmati rice (20 to 25 minutes for long-grain rice). Remove the pan from heat and let it stand, covered, for 5 minutes. Fluff rice with a fork, remove spices if you wish, and serve.

Per portion: 199 calories, 3.7 g protein, 3.2 g fat, 37.6 g carbohydrates, 0.7 g dietary fibre, 21 mg calcium, 0.3 mg iron

Basmati rice is a fragrant, nutty-flavored rice often used in Indian cooking. Although it is relatively expensive, its flavor is incomparable. Basmati rice can be found in some supermarkets, Indian grocery stores and bulk food stores.

LEMON PEPPERED HOMEFRIES

This recipe takes the guesswork out of making great homefries.

Serves 4

4 medium	potatoes (about 1 ¼ lb)
1 tsp	lemon pepper
½ tsp	Italian seasoning
½ tsp	salt
2 tbsp	olive oil

1.   Preheat oven to 425F and lightly grease a baking sheet. Slice potatoes into ½-inch wedges and toss them in a large bowl with lemon pepper, Italian seasoning, salt and oil.
2.   Arrange potatoes in a single layer on a baking sheet. Bake in preheated oven for 40 to 45 minutes, until they are tender. Turn after 25 minutes. If some of the potatoes stick to the baking sheet, return them to the oven. After 5 to 10 more minutes, try turning again. Serve immediately.

Per portion: 164 calories, 2.2 g protein, 7 g fat, 23.9 g carbohydrates, 2.2 g dietary fibre, 16 mg calcium, 1.4 mg iron. Moderate dietary fibre.

TIPS If you're preparing a lot of potatoes, put them in cold water as soon as they're sliced to prevent the flesh from turning brown.

SAVORY SALSA POTATOES

MW READER RECIPE: Brothers Peter and Chris Neal, who produce Neal Brothers potato chips, gave us this yummy recipe. Their products include nachos, potato chips, salsa and pasta sauces.

Serves 4

3 medium	potatoes (about 1 lb)
½ cup	water
2 tbsp	olive oil
1 tbsp	butter
2 tbsp	finely chopped parsley
1	garlic clove, minced
3	eggs
	Generous pinches of salt and black pepper
	Salsa, Neal Brothers or other chunky brand
	Additional chopped parsley

1. Cut potatoes into matchstick-sized pieces. Bring water, 1 tablespoon olive oil and butter to a boil in a small non-stick skillet. Stir in potatoes. Reduce heat and cook, partially covered, stirring occasionally until potatoes are tender and water has evaporated. (You may have to add extra water during cooking.) Uncover, increase heat and cook potatoes, stirring occasionally, until lightly browned.

2. Toss potatoes with parsley and garlic to coat. Whisk eggs, remaining table-spoon of oil, salt and pepper together until blended. Drizzle egg mixture over top of potato mixture to cover. Cook for 3 minutes, until underside of eggs turns golden brown (eggs should still be runny on top). Meanwhile, preheat broiler and wrap handle of frying pan in foil. Place frying pan under broiler and for about 30 seconds, or just until eggs firm. Cut into wedges. Drizzle with salsa and sprinkle with parsley.

Per portion: 239 calories, 7 g protein, 13.5 g fat, 23.1 g carbohydrates, 1.9 g dietary fibre, 33 mg calcium, 1.7 mg iron.

SWEET POTATO AND ORANGE MASH

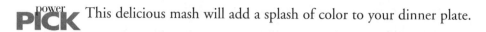

PICK This delicious mash will add a splash of color to your dinner plate.

Serves 6 to 8

3 ½ lb	sweet potatoes, peeled and cut into 1-inch chunks (about 4 or 5)
1 large	orange
½ to ¾ cup	chicken broth
¼ tsp	ground nutmeg
	Salt and black pepper to taste
½ cup	coarsely chopped pecans, preferably toasted (optional)

1. Put potatoes in a large pot; cover with cold water and bring to a boil. Add about 2 teaspoons salt to the water. Reduce heat and simmer, partially covered, until potatoes are very tender — about 30 minutes. Drain well.
2. Meanwhile, finely grate the peel of the orange, then squeeze juice into a measuring cup. Return sweet potatoes to pot and set over low heat. Mash them with the orange peel. Gradually add orange juice and enough chicken broth to reach the desired consistency. You will probably need most of the broth. Add nutmeg, salt and pepper to taste. Fold in pecans.

Per portion: 237 calories, 3.8 g protein, 5.6 g fat, 44.2 g carbohydrates, 4.8 g dietary fibre, 40 mg calcium, 1.2 mg iron, 23 mcg folacin. Excellent source of vitamin C. Good source of vitamin B6. High in dietary fibre.

To toast pecans, spread them in a small ungreased frying pan set over medium heat. Stirring frequently, toast pecans for 4 to 6 minutes or until fragrant. Watch carefully as nuts can burn very quickly.

GARLIC POTATO MASH

Garlic adds the punch to these marvelous mashed potatoes.

Serves 8

6	baking potatoes, peeled and cut into 1-inch chunks
6	whole garlic cloves, peeled
½ cup	buttermilk
2 tbsp	butter
	Salt and pepper to taste

1. Put potatoes in a large pot, cover with cold water and bring to a boil. Add about 2 teaspoons salt to the water. Reduce heat and simmer, partially covered, for about 10 minutes. Add garlic and continue to simmer until potatoes are very tender — about 25 minutes.

2. Drain potatoes, reserving about ¼ cup of the cooking water in the saucepan. Put potatoes and garlic in a ricer and press into the saucepan set over low heat. Stir in buttermilk and butter until potatoes are smooth. If necessary, thin with a bit more buttermilk. Taste and add a generous amount of salt and pepper.

Per portion: 136 calories, 2.7 g protein, 3.2 g fat, 25 g carbohydrates,
1.7 g dietary fibre, 32 mg calcium, 0.4 mg iron, 11 mcg folacin. Good source
of vitamin B6.

If you don't have a potato ricer (available in cooking stores), mash potatoes with buttermilk and butter by hand or with a food mill. For extra speed, use an electric beater. Do not use a food processor; potatoes become gluey and sticky in texture.

MICROWAVED POTATO AND TOMATO CASSEROLE

 A boon to the busy cook — this casserole can be ready in a flash.

 Serves 6

4 medium	unpeeled washed potatoes, cut into 1-inch chunks
2 medium	tomatoes, chopped
1 small	onion, finely chopped
1 tbsp	olive oil
1 tsp	dried leaf basil
½ tsp	dried leaf oregano
½ tsp	salt
	Freshly ground black pepper to taste

1. Stir all ingredients together in a microwave-safe bowl. Cover with plastic wrap, leaving a slight opening to allow steam to escape, and microwave on high for 5 to 7 minutes. Check to see if potatoes are tender. Microwave a few more minutes if necessary. Add more salt to taste.

Per serving: 136 calories, 2.7 g protein, 2.5 g fat, 26.3 g carbohydrates,
2.9 g dietary fibre, 20 mg calcium, 1.6 mg iron, 15 mcg folacin. Good source
of vitamin C and vitamin B6. Moderate amount of dietary fibre.

Microwave cooking time will vary depending on the type of potatoes used, size of chunks and size of microwave dish.

LEMON CHIVE POTATOES

Herbs and lemon add the perfect touch to mild-tasting potatoes.

Serves 4

1 ½ lbs	mini potatoes, either red or white, washed
1 tbsp	butter
2 tsp	lemon juice
½ tsp	lemon peel
2 tbsp	chopped chives or green onions
½ tsp	salt
	Freshly ground black pepper

1. Put potatoes in a large pot of cold salted water. Bring to a boil, and cook potatoes just until tender, 8 to 10 minutes (depending on size of potatoes).
2. Drain potatoes and set them aside. Turn off heat and put pan back on the element. Melt butter in the pan. Stir in lemon juice, peel and chives. Return potatoes to the pan; toss with salt and pepper.

Per portion: 149 calories, 2.9 g protein, 3 g fat, 28.4 g carbohydrates, 2.4 g dietary fibre, 17 mg calcium, 1.2 mg iron, 15 mcg folacin. Good source of vitamin C and vitamin B6. Moderate in dietary fibre.

If you can't find small potatoes, cut regular-sized potatoes into 1-inch chunks or 2-inch rounds, and proceed with recipe. Store potatoes in a cool, dark place where air can circulate around them. They should not be stored in the refrigerator because potato starch turns to sugar, causing the potato flesh to darken when cooked. Potatoes turn green when exposed to light. Discard green potatoes.

ORANGE GLAZED CARROTS

A little sweetness goes a long way when you're trying to make vegetables more appealing.

Serves 4

5 medium	carrots, cut into ¼-inch slices (about 2 ½ cups)
1 tbsp	butter
2 tbsp	orange marmalade
Pinch	ground nutmeg
	Salt and black pepper to taste

1. In a medium saucepan, cover carrots with water. Add a pinch of salt. Bring to a boil and cook until tender-crisp, about 5 minutes. Drain well, then set aside.

2. In the same saucepan, melt butter over medium-low heat. Stir in marmalade and nutmeg, cooking until marmalade is melted. Return carrots to saucepan, and toss to coat evenly with glaze. Add salt and pepper to taste. Serve with pork tenderloin, chicken or beef.

Per portion: 93 calories, 1.1 g protein, 3 g fat, 16.7 g carbohydrates, 3 g dietary fibre, 33 mg calcium, 0.6 mg iron

Looking for a tasty way to turn your family on to parsnips? Just substitute parsnips for the carrots in this recipe and you'll have them begging for seconds. You may need to cook the parsnips a minute longer.

SAUTÉED PEAS WITH LEMON AND FRESH MINT

Plant a window box with fresh herbs and you'll have a fragrant kitchen all year long.

Serves 4

2 tsp	butter
2 tbsp	lemon juice
½ tsp	finely grated lemon peel
2 cups	fresh peas
2 tbsp	finely chopped fresh mint
	Salt and pepper to taste

1. Melt butter with lemon juice and grated peel in a medium-sized frying pan over medium heat. Add peas and cook, stirring occasionally, just until tender. Stir in mint, salt and pepper. Serve immediately.

Per serving: 79 calories, 3.8 g protein, 2.1 g fat, 12 g carbohydrates, 4.7 g dietary fibre, 20 mg calcium, 1.1 mg iron

If fresh peas aren't available, frozen peas will also work well in this recipe (no need to thaw). Fresh dill or parsley can be substituted for the mint.

TANGY BRAISED RED CABBAGE

MW READER RECIPE: Anne Taylor — like a lot of us — doesn't eat as many vegetables as she thinks she should because plain boiled seems boring, and doing something fancy takes too much time. "I came up with this recipe because cabbage doesn't go bad if it sits in my fridge, and I don't have to stand by the stove while it cooks. Plus, I love anything that has soy sauce and sesame oil!"

Serves 6

1 tbsp	vegetable oil
1	red onion, thinly sliced
2 large	garlic cloves, minced
8 cups	red cabbage, shredded (about ½ medium cabbage)
½ cup	chicken broth
2 tbsp	red wine vinegar
2 tbsp	soy sauce
	Pinch of chili flakes
	Dark Oriental sesame oil to taste

1. In a large frying pan, heat oil over medium heat. Add onion and garlic, and cook until onion is soft, about 5 minutes.
2. Add cabbage, broth, vinegar, soy sauce and chili flakes. Toss well to combine. Cover and cook over medium heat until cabbage is tender, about 15 minutes, stirring halfway through cooking. Toss with a few drops of sesame oil. Taste, then add more if you like. Great with pork or lamp chops.

Per portion: 60 calories, 2 g protein, 3 g fat, 7.4 g carbohydrates, 2.5 g dietary fibre, 42 mg calcium, 0.6 mg iron

GRILLED BELGIAN ENDIVE

Belgian endive is a salad green sold in the produce section of your supermarket. Often used in salads, this slightly bitter-tasting vegetable is delicious barbecued.

Serves 4

2	Belgian endives
¼ cup	lemon juice
2 tbsp	olive oil
½ tsp	salt and freshly ground black pepper

1. Preheat barbecue to medium. Wash endives and discard any outer leaves that are discolored. Slice endives in half lengthwise, leaving base intact.
2. Stir lemon juice with olive oil, salt and pepper, and brush endive halves with the mixture. Place cut side down on greased grill. Continue to baste with lemon juice mixture, turning frequently during cooking. Cooking will take 12 to 15 minutes. Endive should be fork-tender when cooked. This recipe can easily be doubled or tripled.

Per portion: 71 calories, 0.5 g protein, 6.9 g fat, 2.8 g carbohydrates, 0.1 g dietary fibre, 12 mg calcium, 0.3 mg iron

 To prevent smaller vegetables from slipping through your barbecue rack, use a smaller-spaced barbecue grill. Grease it lightly, then place it directly on the rack. It's ideal for fish and shellfish too. You'll find them in cookware stores, some hardware stores and some supermarkets.

BBQ CORN-ON-THE-COB AND TOPPERS

MW READER RECIPE: Jane Mullen wrote to ask us how to barbecue corn-on-the-cob. Here's the easiest way (we've also included some easy toppers for a change of pace).

Serves 1
To grill corn-on-the-cob
Carefully peel back husks from corn and remove and discard silky threads. Then rewrap outer husks around corn. (Tie husk ends together with string if necessary). Soak corn in husks in water for 1 hour. Preheat barbecue to medium-high. Place corn on grill, turning frequently, and barbecue for 12 to 15 minutes. Brush husks with water during barbecuing.

Toppers
Start with ¼ cup soft butter and mix in one of the following combinations:
1. Cheddar and chili: 2 tbsp grated cheddar cheese, ½ tsp chili powder, pinches of salt and black pepper to taste.
2. Lemon chive: 1 ½ tbsp finely chopped fresh chives, 2 tsp lemon juice, 1 tsp chopped lemon peel, pinches of salt and black pepper to taste.
3. Spicy curry: 1 ½ tsp medium-hot curry powder, a couple of dashes of Tabasco, pinches of salt and black pepper to taste.
4. Fresh herb: 2 tbsp finely chopped fresh mixed herbs (here's a chance to really experiment), pinches of salt and black pepper to taste.

Per portion: 246 calories, 6.1 g protein, 8.1 g fat, 45.3 g carbohydrates, 6.7 g dietary fibre, 6 mg calcium, 1.1 mg iron.

POTATO CURRY

Potatoes are an excellent way to add more fibre to your diet.

Serves 4

3 medium	potatoes (about 1 lb)
1 tbsp	vegetable oil
½ cup	finely chopped onion (about 1 small)
2	garlic cloves, minced
2 tsp	finely chopped ginger
½ tsp	cumin seeds
2 medium	tomatoes, chopped and preferably peeled
1 tsp	curry powder, preferably medium or hot
½ tsp	salt
	Black pepper to taste

1. Cut potatoes in half and put them in a saucepan of cold salted water. Bring to a boil and cook, partially covered, just until barely tender — 10 to 15 minutes. Do not overcook or they will be mushy. Cut into 1-inch cubes.

2. Heat oil in a large frying pan over medium heat. Add onion, garlic, ginger and cumin seeds. Cook, stirring frequently, until onion is soft. Add tomatoes, curry powder and salt; reduce heat and cover. Cook, stirring occasionally, until tomatoes have softened. Add potato cubes to tomato mixture. Cook, covered, stirring occasionally, until potatoes are hot and tomato mixture is stew-like in consistency. Depending on the juiciness of the tomatoes, you may need to uncover the pan and cook for a few more minutes to thicken tomato mixture. Add pepper. Taste and add more salt if necessary.

Per portion: 140 calories, 2.7 g protein, 3.8 g fat, 25.3 g carbohydrates, 2.6 g dietary fibre, 26 mg calcium, 1 mg iron. Moderate in dietary fibre.

To peel tomatoes, use a sharp knife to score an X at the base of the tomato. Bring a saucepan of water to boil; plunge the tomatoes into the water for 15 to 30 seconds. Immediately drain and rinse them under cold running water. When tomatoes are cool, peel. This recipe works just as well using leftover potatoes.

ASPARAGUS WITH
TOASTED PARMESAN BREAD CRUMBS

Welcome the flavors of spring with this great dish.

Serves 4

1 lb	asparagus
1 ½ tbsp	butter
1	garlic clove, minced
¼ cup	dry bread crumbs
2 tbsp	finely grated Parmesan cheese
1 tbsp	finely chopped parsley
	Salt and pepper to taste

1. Trim tough ends of asparagus. Using a large, wide frying pan, cook asparagus in about ½ inch water just until tender — 3 to 5 minutes.
2. Meanwhile, melt butter in a small frying pan over medium-high heat. Add garlic and cook about 30 seconds, just until soft. Add bread crumbs and cook, stirring frequently until toasted and golden brown — 5 to 7 minutes. Transfer the mixture to a small bowl and stir in Parmesan, parsley, salt and pepper. Cool slightly.
3. Drain asparagus and serve topped with Parmesan bread crumbs.

Per serving: 100 calories, 4.3 g protein, 5.8 g fat, 8.8 g carbohydrates,
1.5 g dietary fibre, 72 mg calcium, 0.9 mg iron

When choosing asparagus, look for straight spears with tightly closed green or purple tips. Wash under cold running water to remove any grit, then snap off or trim the tough woody ends. Asparagus is best cooked right away but can be stored for 2 to 3 days in the refrigerator. Store asparagus upright (stem side down) in water, or wrap ends with damp paper towel and plastic wrap.

FRESH FRUIT SALSA

Salsa adds a quick and colorful touch to a great variety of dishes.

Makes 1 ½ cups

1	seedless orange
1	ripe mango, peeled, pitted and cut into ½-inch pieces
2	kiwi fruit, peeled and cut into ½-inch pieces
1 tsp	granulated sugar
2 to 3 tsp	seeded minced jalapeño pepper
2 tbsp	finely chopped fresh mint

1. Finely grate peel from orange. Using a very sharp knife, remove all the white pith. Cut orange between membranes into segments, then chop into ½-inch pieces.

2. In a small bowl, stir orange and orange peel with the remaining ingredients. Taste and add more finely chopped jalapeño if you like. Cover and refrigerate for at least 4 hours, stirring occasionally. Serve with chicken, turkey, fish, shrimp or pork.

Per tbsp: 14 calories, 0.2 g protein, 0.1 g fat, 3.6 g carbohydrates,
0.6 g dietary fibre, 6 mg calcium, 0.1 mg iron

TIPS It's a good idea to wear latex gloves when seeding and mincing hot peppers. And be sure to avoid touching your eyes or face after handling the veins and seeds, which can burn skin.

AVOCADO AND PEACH SALSA

You can prepare this salsa a day before it's needed by combining all ingredients except the avocado. Prepare and add the avocado just before serving.

Makes 2 cups

1	ripe avocado, pitted, peeled and cut into ½-inch pieces
3	drained unsweetened canned peach halves, or 1 large fresh peach, peeled and cut into ½-inch pieces
½ cup	chopped red pepper
2	green onions, thinly sliced

1 ½ tbsp	lime juice
1 tbsp	olive oil
2 tbsp	finely chopped coriander or parsley
½ tsp	hot chili flakes
	Generous pinches of salt

1. Stir together all ingredients in a medium-sized bowl. Serve immediately before the avocado begins to turn brown. Delicious with chicken or pork.

Per tbsp: 18 calories, 0.2 g protein, 1.4 g fat, 1.6 g carbohydrates, 0.3 g dietary fibre, 2 mg calcium, 0.1 mg iron

CUCUMBER AND MELON SALSA

There is no need to peel or seed English cucumbers. However, regular cucumbers have seeds that you may wish to remove.

Makes 2 ¼ cups

½ cup	chopped English cucumber
½ cup	chopped cantaloupe
½ cup	chopped honeydew melon
1	tomato, seeded and chopped
2	green onions, finely chopped
1 to 2	limes
2 tbsp	olive oil
1 ½ tsp	ground cumin
½ tsp	liquid honey or granulated sugar
	Generous pinches of salt and cayenne

1. Stir together cucumber, cantaloupe, honeydew melon, tomato and green onions in a medium-sized bowl until combined.
2. Finely grate peel from 1 lime, then squeeze out 3 tablespoons of juice (it may be necessary to use the second lime). Stir lime juice and peel with oil, cumin, honey, salt and cayenne until mixed. Toss with cucumber mixture. Taste and add more salt if necessary. Serve with fish or shrimp.

Per tbsp: 10 calories, 0.1 g protein, 0.8 g fat, 0.9 g carbohydrates, 0.1 g dietary fibre, 2 mg calcium, 0.1 mg iron

RICE AND BEANS

This rich and hearty dish is terrific served with a barbecued main course.

Serves 4 to 6

2 tsp	vegetable oil
1	onion, finely chopped
1	small green pepper, cored, seeded and finely chopped
½ cup	finely chopped celery
2	garlic cloves, minced
1 tsp	dried mustard
½ tsp each	dried thyme and oregano
1	bay leaf
¼ to ½ tsp	cayenne
2 cups	chicken broth
2 tbsp	tomato paste
1 cup	long-grain rice
1	19-oz can black beans or kidney beans, rinsed and drained
	Salt to taste

1.   Heat oil in a large saucepan over medium heat. Add onion, green pepper, celery and garlic. Cook, stirring, until onion softens. Stir in mustard, thyme, oregano, bay leaf and ¼ teaspoon cayenne.

2.   Add chicken broth and tomato paste, stirring to dissolve tomato paste. Add rice and beans and bring to a boil. Cover and simmer over low heat for about 25 minutes, or until liquid is absorbed. Add remaining cayenne if you wish, and salt to taste.

Per portion: 359 calories, 15.3 g protein, 4.2 g fat, 65.0 g carbohydrates, 7.5 g dietary fibre, 67 mg calcium, 3.2 mg iron, 155 mcg folacin. Excellent source of folacin. Good source of vitamin C, vitamin B6 and iron. Very high in dietary fibre.

This can be made a day ahead. To reheat, add a couple of tablespoons of broth or water, cover, and place over low heat. It can also be frozen, once it has cooled; when reheating, add a little broth or water.

SAUTÉED DANDELION GREENS

Dandelion greens have a slightly bitter taste. As a general rule, the smaller the leaf, the less bitter. Dandelion greens can also be used in salads.

Serves 4

4 strips	bacon, cut into ½-inch pieces
1 large	bunch dandelion greens, cut into 2-inch pieces
¼ cup	chicken broth
	Salt and freshly ground black pepper
2 tbsp	chopped toasted hazelnuts (optional)

1.   Cook bacon in a large frying pan over medium heat until fairly crisp. Remove with a slotted spoon or lifter, leaving fat in the pan, and set aside on paper towels to absorb the fat. Discard all but 1 tablespoon fat from the frying pan.

2.   Add dandelion leaves to the fat and cook just until leaves are wilted. Add chicken broth, and cook, covered, for 3 to 5 minutes, stirring occasionally. Taste and add salt and pepper.

3.   Remove to a small serving dish and sprinkle with bacon and hazelnuts, if using. Serve over lightly fried slices of polenta. Polenta can be purchased ready-made in supermarkets or Italian food stores.

Per portion: 122 calories, 5.5 g protein, 7.5 g fat, 10.5 g carbohydrates, 4.7 g dietary fibre, 228 mg calcium, 3.1 mg iron. Excellent source of vitamin C, vitamin B6, calcium and iron; high in dietary fibre.

SPICED SQUASH AND APPLE PURÉE

Harvest vegetables, like apples and squash, give you the taste of autumn.

Serves 4 to 6

1 tbsp	butter
1 small	onion
2	garlic cloves, minced
1 ½ tsp	curry powder
3 lb	butternut squash, peeled, seeded and cut into small chunks (about 4 ½ cups)
1	apple, peeled, cored and coarsely chopped
⅔ cup	apple juice
1 ½ tbsp	honey
1 tsp	lemon juice
	Salt and cayenne pepper

1. In a large wide frying pan, heat butter over medium heat. Add onion, garlic and curry powder. Cook until onion is soft, about 5 minutes.
2. Add squash, apple and ½ cup apple juice, tossing to combine with onion. Cover and cook over medium heat until squash is very tender, 10 to 15 minutes. Stir occasionally during cooking. If liquid completely evaporates, add remaining apple juice.
3. Remove to a food processor or blender, and purée in batches until smooth. Stir in honey, lemon juice, salt and cayenne to taste. Serve with turkey or lamb.

Per portion (6 servings): 108 calories, 1.2 g protein, 2.2 g fat, 23.3 g carbohydrates, 3.3 g dietary fibre, 43 mg calcium, 1.0 mg iron

If you're short on time, look for fresh, pre-peeled, precut squash in your supermarket's vegetable section. Or check the frozen food section for cubed squash.

APPLE RICE SIDE DISH

Apples and currants make this rice a sweet sensation. Serve it with chicken or pork.

Serves 4

10 oz	undiluted chicken broth or 1 ¼ cups canned chicken stock
½ cup	water
½ tsp	each rubbed sage and thyme
½ tsp	salt
1 cup	long-grain white rice
½	firm apple, such as Spy or Granny Smith
2	thinly sliced green onions
2 tbsp	currants
	Freshly ground black pepper

1. Bring broth, water, sage, thyme and salt to a boil in a medium-sized saucepan. Stir in rice. Cover and reduce heat to low. Gently simmer rice, still covered, for 20 minutes.

2. Meanwhile, peel apple and cut it into ¼-inch pieces (you should have about ½ cup). Gently stir apple, green onion and currants into rice. Continue to cook rice, covered, for 5 more minutes or until liquid is completely absorbed. Stir in black pepper to taste.

Per portion: 215 calories, 7.2 g protein, 1.2 g fat, 43 g carbohydrates, 1.4 g dietary fibre, 34 mg calcium, 1 mg iron.

PERKY POTATOES

MW READER RECIPE: Mary Williams, from St. Catharines, Ontario, is an enthusiastic cook who enjoys experimenting with exotic ingredients. This recipe is one of her favourites, even though it's been around for years. Whenever she makes it for a potluck or buffet, it's the first to go. "It's really easy. Kids and adults love it, and it freezes and reheats well." What more can you ask?

Serves 12

1	2-lb bag frozen hash brown potatoes (do not thaw)
2 cups	light or regular sour cream
1 ¼ cups	grated old cheddar cheese
½ cup	chopped green onions (about 5 onions)
1	10-oz can undiluted cream of chicken soup
1 tsp	salt
½ tsp	black pepper
1 ¼ to 1 ½ cups	crushed cornflakes
¼ cup	melted butter

1. Preheat oven to 350F and grease a 9 x 13-inch casserole dish. In a large bowl, mix hash browns, sour cream, cheddar cheese, green onions, chicken soup, salt and pepper until well combined. Turn the mixture into casserole dish.
2. Sprinkle cornflakes evenly over top so that casserole is covered. Drizzle with melted butter. Bake for 45 minutes or until casserole is hot.

Per portion: 241 calories, 8 g protein, 12.3 g fat, 25.3 g carbohydrates, 1.5 g dietary fibre, 182 mg calcium, 2 mg iron

PERFECT PASTAS

Pastas are perfect family food. Fast and easy to prepare, they're a great choice for cooks on the go. In minutes you can combine veggies, meat and grains in one dish that will feed everyone from those with the heartiest of appetites to the pickiest eater.

We've put together our favourite pasta recipes from the last five years, including some terrific Reader Recipes and a sensational Spaghetti Sauce. Whether it's Creamy Linguini or Quick Chili Lasagna, there's a pasta here to suit every taste.

TORTELLINI WITH BACON AND ROSEMARY SAUCE

Bacon and rosemary are a great taste combination. You'll love them tossed with cheese tortellini.

Serves 6

2 strips	bacon, cut into small pieces
1	onion, chopped
2	cloves garlic, minced
1	28-oz can plum tomatoes, including juice
½ cup	dry white wine (optional)
1 tbsp	chopped fresh rosemary (or 1 ½ tsp dried rosemary, crumbled)
	Generous pinch cayenne
	Salt and pepper to taste
2	350-g pkgs frozen or fresh tortellini with cheese
½ cup	freshly grated Parmesan cheese

1.   In a large saucepan, cook bacon until crisp. Remove bacon with a slotted spoon and set aside on a paper towel. Reduce heat to medium-low; add onion and garlic. Cook for a couple of minutes until onion is soft. Add tomatoes and juice, crushing tomatoes with the back of a spoon. Add wine, rosemary and cayenne; bring to a boil. Reduce heat and simmer, uncovered, for 25 to 30 minutes, stirring occasionally until mixture is quite thick. Add salt and pepper to taste.

2.   Meanwhile, cook tortellini, following package instructions, until just tender (use shortest cooking time if there is a range). The tortellini will soften when reheated. Toss sauce with tortellini and turn into a casserole dish. Sprinkle with reserved bacon and Parmesan.

3.   Cover and refrigerate for up to two days. To reheat, preheat oven to 350F. Bake, covered, for 20 minutes; uncover and continue to bake for 10 to 15 minutes more, or until casserole is hot.

Per portion: 408 calories, 19.2 g protein, 10.3 g fat, 60 g carbohydrates, 4.4 g dietary fibre, 263 mg calcium, 2.8 mg iron, 29 mcg folacin. Good source of calcium, iron and zinc. High in dietary fibre.

ORZO, CHICKEN AND VEGETABLE GRATIN

Orzo is a small, rice-shaped pasta. It's available in most supermarkets but you can substitute any small pasta.

Serves 4

2 cups	orzo
2 tsp	olive oil
1	onion, diced
2	carrots, diced
1 stalk	celery, diced
1 small	zucchini, diced
3 cups	bite-sized pieces of cooked chicken
½ cup each	chicken broth and milk
⅔ cup	freshly grated Parmesan cheese
¼ cup	finely chopped parsley
	Salt and pepper to taste
3 tbsp	fresh bread crumbs

1. Cook orzo according to package directions. Heat oil in a large saucepan over medium heat. Add onion, carrots, celery and zucchini, and cook, stirring, until vegetables are fairly tender — about 2 minutes.
2. Stir in chicken, chicken broth, milk, ½ cup of the Parmesan cheese, half of the parsley, salt and pepper to taste. Turn into a casserole dish. Stir together bread crumbs, remaining Parmesan and parsley, and more salt and pepper. Sprinkle over orzo mixture.
3. Refrigerate, covered, for up to two days before cooking. To heat pasta, pre-heat oven to 350F. Bake, covered, for about 30 minutes. Uncover and continue to bake for about 15 minutes more, or until pasta is hot and bread crumbs are a deep golden brown.

Per portion: 672 calories, 50.9 g protein, 17.5 g fat, 74.8 g carbohydrates, 5.8 g dietary fibre, 330 mg calcium, 3.4 mg iron, 46 mcg folacin. Excellent source of vitamin A, vitamin B6 and vitamin B12, calcium and zinc. Good source of iron. High in dietary fibre.

To make fresh bread crumbs, put a couple of slices of bread in a food processor; pulse until coarse crumbs form.

RATATOUILLE PASTA

Serving a vegetarian pasta mid-week is a great way to give your family a break from meat.

Serves 6

1 tbsp	olive oil
1	unpeeled medium eggplant, chopped (about 4 cups)
2 small	zucchini, sliced lengthwise, then crossways into small pieces. (about 3 cups)
½ lb	sliced mushrooms (about 3 cups)
1 large	onion, sliced into rings
1 each	red and green pepper, cut into strips
4	garlic cloves, minced
1 tsp	Italian seasoning
¼ tsp	chili flakes
1	28-oz can plum tomatoes, including juice
1	450-g pkg penne, fusilli or rotini
	Grated Parmesan cheese (optional)

1.   Heat oil in a very large wide frying pan or saucepan over medium heat. Add all the vegetables (except plum tomatoes), garlic, Italian seasoning and chili flakes. Cook for a couple of minutes, stirring.
2.   Add tomatoes and their juice. Stir well, crushing tomatoes with the back of a spoon. Cover and simmer mixture for 30 minutes, stirring occasionally. Uncover and continue to simmer, stirring occasionally, for 20 to 30 minutes more, until mixture is fairly thick.
3.   Meanwhile, cook pasta according to package directions. Drain well and toss with sauce. Cool slightly, then refrigerate, covered. The pasta mixture will keep well for up to three days before its final cooking. When you're ready to use it, preheat oven to 350F and bake, covered, for 30 to 40 minutes, or until pasta is hot. Serve with Parmesan.

Per portion: 382 calories, 12.9 g protein, 4.4 g fat, 74.9 g carbohydrates, 8.7 g dietary fibre, 75 mg calcium, 3 mg iron, 52 mcg folacin. Excellent source of vitamin C. Good source of vitamin A, vitamin B6, iron and zinc. Very high in dietary fibre.

TURKEY, FENNEL AND SUNDRIED TOMATO FUSILLI

This make-ahead pasta supper can easily be frozen. To reheat it, thaw it overnight in the refrigerator, then follow the steps for baking.

Serves 6

1 lb	extra lean ground turkey or chicken
1 small	fennel bulb, chopped (3 to 4 cups)
1	red or green pepper, chopped
1	onion, chopped
2	large garlic cloves, minced
¼ cup	sundried tomatoes in oil, rinsed and sliced into slivers
1 ½ tsp	dried basil
	Finely grated peel of 1 orange
1	28-oz can plum tomatoes, including juice
¾	of a 450-g pkg fusilli, macaroni or rotini
1 cup	finely diced mozzarella cheese
	Salt and pepper

1. Cook turkey, fennel, red pepper, onion, garlic, sundried tomatoes, basil and orange peel in a large saucepan over medium heat, stirring frequently to break up meat, until turkey is no longer pink. Add tomatoes and juice. Simmer gently, uncovered, stirring occasionally until sauce thickens slightly — about 15 minutes.
2. Meanwhile, cook pasta according to package directions. Drain well and toss pasta with sauce, cheese, salt and pepper to taste. Serve immediately, or cool slightly, then refrigerate, covered, for up to two days before cooking. To heat pasta, preheat oven to 350F. Bake, covered, for about 30 minutes, or until pasta is hot.

Per portion: 466 calories, 27.7 g protein, 14.4 g fat, 56.7 g carbohydrates, 6.6 g dietary fibre, 194 mg calcium, 2.6 mg iron, 38 mcg folacin. Excellent source of vitamin C, vitamin B6 and zinc. Good source of vitamin A, vitamin B12, calcium and iron. Very high in dietary fibre.

PASTA PRIMAVERA

MW READER RECIPE: Rosa Spada thinks Pasta Primavera is a perfect summer meal. Make it for dinner one night and enjoy any leftovers for a picnic the next day. Rosa loves to cook for her own family and the neighborhood children she looks after.

Serves 4

1 small	bunch broccoli
1	450-g pkg tagliatelle
2 tbsp	olive oil
1 medium	onion, chopped
2 medium	carrots, sliced thinly on the diagonal
2	plum or regular tomatoes, peeled, seeded and coarsely chopped
1 large	red pepper, cut into long thin strips
½ tsp	salt
¼ tsp	chili flakes (optional)

1.   Cut off the broccoli stalks. Discard the tough bottom 2 inches and peel the remaining stalks. Cut them thinly on the diagonal. Cut broccoli into small florets; set both aside.

2.   Bring a large pot of water to a full, rolling boil. Add about 1 tablespoon salt to the water, then add pasta. Cook for about 5 minutes or until pasta is just tender.

3.   Heat oil in a large wide frying pan over medium heat. Add onion and cook for 3 minutes, or just until onion is soft. Add the remaining ingredients and cook, stirring frequently, for about 5 minutes or just until vegetables are tender but not mushy (if necessary, increase heat). Drain pasta well, then toss with vegetable mixture.

Per portion: 550 calories, 18.2 g protein, 9.4 g fat, 99.5 g carbohydrates, 9.6 g dietary fibre, 86 mg calcium, 3 mg iron. A good source of iron. Very high in dietary fibre.

PASTA ALLA CAMPANIOLA

MW READER RECIPE: Mary E. Grieco loves to prepare fresh, simple food from scratch. In summer, she prepares food that's not too heavy and doesn't involve a lot of cooking over a hot stove. Pasta and barbecued vegetable dishes are among her favourites.

Serves 4

2 tbsp	olive oil
2	garlic cloves, coarsely chopped
4 oz	pancetta, chopped
2 medium	zucchini, coarsely chopped (about 3 cups)
12 large	mushrooms, coarsely chopped
8	black or green olives, pitted and chopped
1 tbsp	capers, drained
1	450-g pkg penne pasta
5	plum tomatoes, peeled, seeded and chopped
	Salt and pepper to taste
	Parmesan cheese, preferably Parmigiano-Reggiano

1. Heat oil in a large wide saucepan over medium heat. Add garlic and cook, stirring frequently, for 2 minutes; do not let garlic brown. Remove and discard garlic. Add pancetta to pan and cook, stirring occasionally, for 5 minutes. Drain all but 1 tablespoon fat. Stir in zucchini, mushrooms, olives and capers. Cook, stirring occasionally, until vegetables are tender, for 10 to 15 minutes.
2. Meanwhile, bring a large pot of water to a rolling boil; add about 1 tablespoon salt. Add pasta to the water and cook for 7 to 9 minutes, or just until tender (al dente).
3. While pasta is cooking and when vegetables in the saucepan are soft, add tomatoes to the vegetables. Cook for 5 to 6 minutes, or until tomatoes are soft. Taste and add salt and pepper. Drain pasta and put it on individual serving plates. Spoon sauce over top and serve with Parmesan.

Per portion: 690 calories, 19 g protein, 26.7 fat, 94 g carbohydrates, 8.5 g dietary fibre, 59 mg calcium, 3.7 mg iron. Excellent source of iron. Very high in dietary fibre.

MEDITERRANEAN TUNA PENNE

Adding a hint of lemon to recipes, like this Mediterranean Tuna Penne, is a way of brightening all the flavors in the dish.

Serves 6 to 8

1	450-g pkg penne, rotini or fusilli
1 tsp	olive or vegetable oil
1	onion, chopped
1 cup	diced zucchini
2	garlic cloves, minced
2 tsp	dried leaf basil
1	300-g pkg frozen chopped spinach, thawed
	Finely grated peel and juice of 1 lemon
⅓ cup	chopped parsley
2	19-oz cans stewed tomatoes, preferably Italian
1 cup	crumbled feta cheese or grated cheddar cheese
2	6-oz cans solid white tuna
	(preferably water-packed), drained

1. Cook penne in a large pot of boiling salted water just until tender — about 8 minutes. Meanwhile, heat oil in a large deep frying pan over medium heat. Add onion, zucchini, garlic and basil; cook, stirring, for about 2 minutes. Stir in spinach, lemon peel and juice, and parsley.
2. Once pasta is cooked, drain well. Mix with the spinach mixture in frying pan. Then mix in tomatoes, cheese and tuna until blended. Turn into a large casserole dish and bake, covered, in a preheated 350F oven for about 30 minutes, or until casserole is hot.

Per portion: 475 calories, 27.7 g protein, 8 g fat, 74.8 g carbohydrates, 7.2 g dietary fibre, 248 mg calcium, 3.7 mg iron, 75 mcg folacin. Excellent source of vitamin A, vitamin C, vitamin B6 and vitamin B12 and folacin. Good source of calcium. High in dietary fibre.

PASTA WITH TOMATOES, ARTICHOKES AND OLIVES

Artichokes are a great source of iron.

Serves 4

1	170-mL jar quartered marinated artichoke hearts
1 medium	onion, finely chopped
4	garlic cloves, minced
2 medium	carrots, sliced
1 small	orange
1	28-oz can plum tomatoes with juice
1 tsp	basil
½ tsp each	thyme, oregano and salt
Pinch	chili flakes
1	450-g pkg rotini or penne
⅓ cup	olives (optional)
	Fresh grated Parmesan cheese

1. Put 2 tablespoons of artichoke marinade into a large saucepan. Drain artichokes and discard the remaining marinade. Heat marinade over medium heat. Add onion, garlic and carrots, and sauté for 5 minutes or until slightly soft.
2. Cut the peel from the orange in wide strips, leaving the bitter white pith behind. Add peel to the saucepan along with the juice of the orange, plum tomatoes and their juice, and seasonings. Stir to break up tomatoes. Bring the mixture to a boil, reduce heat and simmer uncovered for 20 to 25 minutes or until mixture has thickened slightly. Stir occasionally.
3. Meanwhile, bring a large pot of water to a boil. Add about a tablespoon of salt. Add pasta. Cook for 8 to 10 minutes or just until pasta is tender but not soft. Drain. Just before serving, remove the orange peel from the sauce and discard it. Stir artichoke hearts and olives into the tomato sauce. Serve pasta topped with sauce and a sprinkling of Parmesan.

Per portion: 574 calories, 18.1 g protein, 9.7 g fat, 105.1 g carbohydrates, 8.9 g dietary fibre, 126 mg calcium, 3.9 mg iron

If you're in a hurry, mix a bottle of meatless tomato sauce with orange peel, artichokes and olives.

CHEESE MANICOTTI WITH TOMATO SAUCE

MW READER RECIPE: Terri Nesbitt, a busy mom with two boys, Ryan and Tyler, plus twins Amy and Kara, often prepares this sauce the night before serving it; she finds that flavors blend overnight.

Serves 6

1 tbsp	olive oil
1	onion, diced
4	garlic cloves, minced
1 medium	zucchini, cut into ¼-inch pieces
1	red or green pepper, cut into ¼-inch pieces
1 oz each	crushed tomatoes and plum tomatoes, including juice
¼ cup	finely grated Parmesan or Romano cheese
2 tbsp	dried tarragon
1 tbsp	Italian herb seasoning
2 tsp	granulated sugar
½ tsp	Tabasco
	Generous pinch salt, black pepper and ground cinnamon
1	300-g pkg frozen chopped spinach, thawed and drained, and squeezed to remove water
3 ¼ cups	grated mozzarella cheese (about 12 oz)
475 g	ricotta cheese
1	225-g pkg manicotti (about 14 manicotti), cooked

1. Heat oil in a large saucepan over medium heat. Add onion, garlic, zucchini and red pepper. Cook for 5 minutes; add tomatoes, Parmesan, 1 tablespoon of tarragon, Italian herb seasoning, sugar, Tabasco, salt, pepper and cinnamon. Bring to a boil. Reduce heat; simmer for 1 hour, stirring occasionally.

2. Put spinach in a bowl with 2 cups of the grated mozzarella, ricotta, remaining tarragon, salt and pepper to taste. Mix until well combined. Stuff the filling into cooked manicotti in equal portions.

3. Spread 1 cup of the sauce over the bottom of a 9 x 13-inch casserole. In a single layer, place the stuffed manicotti on the sauce. Spoon the remaining sauce over manicotti. Sprinkle with remaining mozzarella. Bake in preheated 350F oven for 35 to 40 minutes, or until hot.

Per portion: 257 calories, 14.1 g protein, 13 g fat, 22.1 g carbohydrates, 2.8 g dietary fibre, 310 mg calcium, 1.6 mg iron. Excellent source of calcium.

CHICKEN AND TOMATO CREAMY LINGUINI

Simple and savory — this dish is sure to please.

Serves 4

2 tsp	vegetable or olive oil
1	onion, chopped
1	carrot, finely chopped
2	garlic cloves, minced
1	28-oz can plum tomatoes
1 tsp	basil
½ tsp	oregano
	Pinch each salt and chili flakes
1	450-g pkg linguini
1	160-mL can 2% evaporated partly skimmed milk
2 tsp	cornstarch
2 cups	cubed cooked leftover chicken

1. Heat oil in a medium saucepan over medium heat. Add onion, carrot and garlic; cook for about 3 minutes. Add tomatoes and their juice, basil, oregano, salt and chili flakes. Crush tomatoes with a potato masher. Bring to a boil and boil uncovered, stirring occasionally, for 15 to 20 minutes until thickened.
2. Meanwhile, bring a large pot of salted water to a boil. Add pasta and cook, stirring occasionally, until pasta is cooked. Drain well. Stir evaporated milk with cornstarch; stir into tomato sauce. Bring to a boil, stirring continuously, and add chicken. Cook until heated through.

Per portion: 672 calories, 4 g protein, 10.9 g fat, 102.2 g carbohydrates, 7.8 g dietary fibre, 222 mg calcium, 4 mg iron. Excellent source of iron. Good source of vitamin C and calcium. Very high in dietary fibre.

Evaporated milk has 78% less fat than whipping cream, although nothing beats the taste of real whipping cream. When you're watching your fat intake, evaporated milk makes a great substitute.

SENSATIONAL SPAGHETTI SAUCE

Looking for a great-tasting hearty homemade spaghetti sauce? Here's one the whole family will enjoy — guaranteed!

Makes about 11 cups

1 lb	ground beef
½ lb	ground pork
½ lb	ground veal
1 tbsp	olive oil
1	Spanish onion, chopped
4	garlic cloves, minced
2 large	carrots, thinly sliced
1 large	stalk celery (including leaves)
1	red or green pepper, cored and finely chopped
½ lb	mushrooms, sliced
3	28-oz cans plum tomatoes, including juice
3	bay leaves
2 tbsp	finely chopped Italian parsley
1 ½ tbsp	leaf thyme
1 ½ tbsp	leaf basil
1 tbsp	leaf oregano
1 tsp	leaf rosemary
1 ½ tsp	salt
½ tsp each	black pepper and chili flakes

1.   Cook ground beef, pork and veal in a large wide saucepan over medium heat, stirring frequently until meat is no longer pink. Using a slotted spoon, remove meat to a bowl. Drain all fat from the pan and return pan to medium heat.

2.   Put the oil in the pan, then add onion, garlic, carrots, celery, red pepper and mushrooms. Cook, stirring occasionally, for 8 to 10 minutes until vegetables are tender. Return the meat to the saucepan along with remaining ingredients. Using a spoon, press the plum tomatoes against the side of the pan to crush them slightly.

3.   Bring to a boil, stirring occasionally. Reduce the heat and simmer uncovered, stirring occasionally, for 1 ¼ to 1 ½ hours until slightly thickened. Three-quarters of the way through the cooking, taste and add more seasonings if necessary. Serve over your favourite pasta.

Per cup: 219 calories, 18.6 g protein, 10 g fat, 15 g carbohydrates,
3.7 g dietary fibre, 95 mg calcium, 3.5 mg iron

TIPS Spaghetti sauce will keep well for up to three days if covered and refrigerated. You can also freeze it. Keep in mind, though, that freezing can affect flavor, so be sure to taste the sauce after thawing and reheating. You may need
to boost the flavor with additional herbs and spices.

SPICY CHICKEN AND RED PEPPER PENNE

MW READER RECIPE: Carole Martin, owner of Purple Sage Gourmet
Foods in Calgary, created this great rush-hour recipe for her children
when they were toddlers.

Serves 4

1	450-g pkg penne
1 tbsp	olive oil
4	boneless, skinless chicken breasts, cut into thin strips
2	red peppers, seeded and sliced into lengthwise strips
	(you can substitute mushrooms or broccoli)
½ cup	chicken broth
¼ cup	whipping cream
½ tsp	hot pepper sauce
¼ cup	chopped fresh basil or parsley
	Salt and pepper to taste

1. Bring a large pot of salted water to a boil. Cook pasta according to package
directions.
2. Meanwhile, heat oil in a large non-stick frying pan over medium heat. Add
chicken and cook until lightly browned. Add pepper strips to pan and continue
to cook for a few minutes, stirring frequently. Add chicken broth, stirring up
any brown bits from the bottom of the pan. Add cream and hot pepper sauce.
Reduce heat and simmer, uncovered, 3 to 4 minutes until sauce thickens slightly.
Stir in chopped basil, salt and pepper. Drain pasta and toss with chicken
mixture.

Per serving: 647 calories, 42.9 g protein, 12.3 g fat, 88.3 g carbohydrates,
5.8 g dietary fibre, 54 mg calcium, 3.7 mg iron, 75 mcg folacin. Excellent
source of vitamin A, vitamin C, vitamin B6 and vitamin B12 and folacin.
Good source of calcium. High in dietary fibre.

WILD MUSHROOM PASTA

Porcini and wild mushrooms are expensive but their flavor is unbeatable. To keep the cost down, mix white button mushrooms with the wild varieties.

Serves 2 to 3

1	35-oz pkg porcini mushrooms
½ cup	hot water
1 tbsp	butter
2	garlic cloves, minced
¾ lb	fresh, wild mushrooms (such as oyster, portobello and shiitake), thickly sliced
½	of a 454-g pkg linguine or fettucine
½ cup	dry white wine
2 large	fresh plum tomatoes, diced
½ cup	diced prosciutto
2 tbsp	finely chopped parsley
	Salt and pepper to taste

1. Rinse porcini mushrooms to remove grit. Put them in a small bowl and cover them with the hot water. Set aside for 30 to 40 minutes until soft. Drain mushrooms, reserving the liquid, then chop.
2. Heat butter over medium heat in a large frying pan. Add garlic and cook for 1 minute. Add fresh and porcini mushrooms and cook for a couple of minutes, stirring continuously. Then add reserved liquid to the pan. Cook, stirring occasionally, until liquid from mushrooms has evaporated — about 5 minutes.
3. Meanwhile, bring a large pot of salted water to a boil. Cook pasta just until tender; drain well.
4. Add wine to the pan with mushrooms and cook, stirring occasionally, until wine has nearly evaporated. Stir in tomatoes, prosciutto and parsley and cook just until heated through. Add salt and a generous sprinkling of black pepper.

Per portion: 310 calories, 12.4 g protein, 5.7 g fat, 50.2 g carbohydrates, 4.6 g dietary fibre, 27 mg calcium, 2.4 mg iron. Good source of iron and zinc. High in dietary fibre.

BOW TIES WITH SAUSAGES

MW READER RECIPE: Rod Heyd is a modern stay-at-home dad who enjoys making meals with fun appeal. He told us, "Bow Ties with Sausages can be fun, because the pasta has an interesting shape and we can make up games using all the colors. All we need to complete the meal is a salad and bread."

Serves 4

3	mild Italian sausages
3 cups	thinly sliced zucchini
1	454-g pkg farfalle (bow-tie pasta), preferably three colors
2 tbsp	olive oil
½ cup	grated Parmesan cheese
	Salt and pepper to taste

1. Barbecue sausages over medium heat for about 20 minutes, until cooked. Or put them in a frying pan with about ¼ inch of water. Simmer until the water evaporates, then continue frying until sausages are cooked, about 20 minutes. Slice sausages.
2. Meanwhile, either barbecue or steam zucchini. Bring a large pot of salted water to a boil, and cook pasta until tender. Drain and toss with sausages, zucchini, oil and Parmesan. Add salt and pepper to taste. Serve with bread and carrot sticks.

Per portion: 694 calories, 30.9 g protein, 23.1 g fat, 89 g carbohydrates, 6.1 g dietary fibre, 210 mg calcium, 2.3 mg iron. Good source of calcium and iron, and high in dietary fibre.

Rod suggests substituting broccoli or asparagus for zucchini, and meatballs or chicken for sausage. If you wish to "dekidify" the recipe, try adding hot chili flakes as well as barbecued red pepper strips.

BACON AND TOMATO PENNE

 Pasta cooked al dente should be tender but firm to the bite. Often, children prefer their noodles a little softer — a simple way to make everyone happy is to scoop the "grown-up" pasta out of the pot a few minutes earlier than the kids' noodles.

Serves 4

4 slices	bacon, cut into ½-inch pieces
¾ cup	finely chopped green onions (about 5)
1	carrot, finely chopped
2 large	garlic cloves, minced
1	28-oz can plum tomatoes
½ tsp	Italian seasoning
	Pinch chili flakes
¾	450-g pkg penne
2 tbsp	finely chopped Italian parsley
	Salt and pepper to taste

1. Cook bacon in a large skillet until crisp. Remove with a slotted spoon and set aside. Reduce heat to medium and either drain some of the bacon fat or add oil to pan to make 1 tablespoon. Add green onions, carrot and garlic to the pan and cook, stirring occasionally, until soft — about 3 minutes. Add tomatoes and their juice (crushing with the back of a spoon), Italian seasoning, chili flakes and bacon. Increase heat and boil until sauce has thickened and some of the liquid has evaporated, 13 to 15 minutes.
2. Meanwhile, cook pasta in a large pot of boiling salted water until just tender. Drain well. Add pasta to tomato sauce. Stir in parsley. Taste and add salt and pepper. Serve immediately.

Per serving: 437 calories, 15.1 g protein, 8.5 g fat, 75.6 g carbohydrates, 6.7 g dietary fibre, 95 mg calcium, 3 mg iron. Very high in dietary fibre. Good source of iron and vitamin C.

QUICK BEEF STROGANOFF

 quick &
EASY

Wide egg noodles are perfect for this rich and satisfying dish. Light sour cream cuts down on the fat content, making this a great choice for fat-conscious diets.

Serves 4

1 lb	fast-fry sirloin tip or inside round steak
1 tbsp	vegetable oil
	Salt, black pepper and paprika
½ cup	finely chopped onion
3 cups	sliced mushrooms (about ½ lb)
1 cup	beef broth
2 tbsp	tomato paste
1 tsp	Worcestershire sauce
¼ cup	light or regular sour cream
	Chopped parsley for garnish

1. Trim and discard any visible fat from the meat. Slice steak across the grain into ½-inch-wide strips. Heat oil in a large frying pan over medium-high heat. While oil is heating, lightly sprinkle beef with salt, pepper and paprika, then toss. Put the beef in the pan and stir until cooked through, for about 3 minutes. Remove with a slotted spoon, leaving the juices in the pan.

2. If necessary, add a little more oil to pan. Add onion and mushrooms and cook, stirring continuously, until the vegetables have softened slightly, for about 3 minutes. Add broth, tomato paste and Worcestershire sauce. Whisk until combined. Bring to a boil; boil vigorously until reduced by about half.

3. Reduce heat to a simmer. Return meat to the pan and add sour cream. Stir until combined and heated through. Do not boil or the sour cream will curdle. Taste and add salt and pepper if necessary. Serve over noodles sprinkled with a bit of chopped parsley.

Per portion: 210 calories, 29.1 g protein, 7.2 g fat, 6.5 g carbohydrates, 1.4 g dietary fibre, 47 mg calcium, 3.3 mg iron. Good source of iron.

HARVEST VEGETABLE LASAGNA

This meatless lasagna gets its body from three cheeses and a great combination of veggies.

Serves 6 to 8

10 (approximately) lasagna noodles

1	475-g container ricotta cheese
2	eggs
½ cup	grated Parmesan
	Salt and pepper to taste
1 tbsp	olive oil
1 large	onion, chopped
2	red peppers, seeded and diced
1	green pepper, seeded and diced
1 each	medium zucchini and carrot, diced
3	garlic cloves, minced
2 tsp each	basil and oregano
1	700- to 750-mL jar meatless spaghetti sauce
2 ½ cups	grated mozzarella cheese

1. Cook lasagna noodles according to package directions. Rinse them under cold water and lay them flat in a single layer on waxed paper. In a bowl, stir ricotta with eggs and Parmesan. Add salt and pepper.
2. Heat oil in a frying pan over medium heat. Add onion, peppers, zucchini, carrot, garlic and herbs. Cook uncovered, stirring occasionally, until vegetables are tender. Stir all but 1 cup of the spaghetti sauce into vegetables. Add salt and pepper.
3. Set aside ½ cup mozzarella for the top. Thinly spread ¼ cup of the reserved spaghetti sauce on the bottom of a 9-inch square pan. Cover with four lasagna noodles (overlap slightly), cutting them to fit the pan (save the cut noodles to use for a middle layer). Follow with half of the vegetable sauce. Spread with half of the ricotta and half of the mozzarella. Repeat layering. Top with a final layer of noodles, reserved sauce and reserved mozzarella.
4. Place the pan on a baking sheet and bake, covered, in preheated 350F oven for 50 to 60 minutes (uncover during the last 10 minutes), or until hot in the centre. Let stand for about 10 minutes before cutting.

Per portion: 508 calories, 25 g protein, 24.5 g fat, 47.8 g carbohydrates, 4.9 g dietary fibre, 472 mg calcium, 2.1 mg iron, 47 mcg folacin. Excellent source of vitamin A, vitamin C, vitamin B6, vitamin B12 and calcium. High in dietary fibre.

DELICIOUS MEAT LASAGNA

This recipe takes traditional lasagna and improves it with lots of herbs and spinach.

Serves 8 to 10

15 (approximately)	lasagna noodles
½ lb each	lean ground beef and pork
3 ½ cups	sliced mushrooms (about 8 oz)
1	onion, chopped
2	garlic cloves, minced
1	14-oz can tomato sauce
1	5 ½-oz can tomato paste
⅓ cup	chopped parsley
1 tsp each	dried basil and oregano
	Salt and pepper to taste
1	300-g pkg frozen chopped spinach, squeezed dry
1	475-g container ricotta cheese
1	egg, lightly beaten
¾ cup	grated Parmesan cheese
1 cup	grated mozzarella cheese

1. Cook lasagna noodles according to package directions. Rinse under cold water and lay flat in a single layer on waxed paper.
2. In a frying pan, cook meat, mushrooms, onion and garlic, stirring until meat is no longer pink. Drain fat. Stir in tomato sauce, tomato paste, 1 cup water, herbs, salt and pepper. In a bowl, combine the spinach with ricotta, egg and ½ cup Parmesan.
3. Thinly spread one-quarter of the meat sauce on the bottom of a 9 x 13-inch baking pan. Follow with one-third of the noodles, overlapping slightly. Spread with the spinach and ricotta mixture, followed by a layer of noodles, two-thirds of the meat sauce and mozzarella. Top with the last layer of noodles, remaining meat sauce and Parmesan cheese.
4. Place the pan on a baking sheet and bake, covered, in preheated 350F oven for 1 to 1 ¼ hours (uncover during last 10 minutes), or until hot in the centre. Let stand for about 10 minutes before cutting.

Per portion: 424 calories, 27.1 g protein, 17.8 g fat, 39.5 g carbohydrates, 4.2 g dietary fibre, 328 mg calcium, 3 mg iron, 51 mcg folacin. Excellent source of vitamin A, vitamin B12 and calcium. Good source of vitamin B6, folacin and iron. High in dietary fibre.

SAUSAGE AND FENNEL LASAGNA

Italian sausage, fennel and goat's cheese put a delicious twist on an old favourite.

Serves 8 to 10

3	Italian sausages
3 ½ cups	sliced mushrooms (about 8 oz)
1 cup	diced fennel or celery
1	carrot, diced
1	red or green pepper, diced
1	onion, chopped
2	700-mL jars meatless spaghetti sauce
3 cups	grated mozzarella cheese
1	4.5-oz pkg plain goat's cheese
¼ cup	chopped parsley
12 to 15	oven-ready lasagna noodles

1. Remove sausages from their casings. Cook the sausage meat in a frying pan along with mushrooms, fennel, carrot, red pepper and onion, stirring frequently, until sausage is cooked and no longer pink. Drain fat. Add spaghetti sauce and heat until hot. Set aside 1 cup mozzarella. In a bowl, stir together remaining mozzarella, goat's cheese and parsley.

2. Spread one-quarter of the sauce on the bottom of a 9 x 13-inch pan. Arrange four to five uncooked lasagna noodles over sauce, spacing them ½ inch apart. (If necessary, break noodles in half to fit). Spread one-third of remaining sauce over noodles. Using half the cheese mixture, drop small spoonfuls of it randomly over the sauce. Follow with another layer of noodles, half the sauce and the rest of the cheese mixture. Top with the remaining noodles and sauce, making sure noodles are completely covered in sauce. Sprinkle with reserved mozzarella.

3. Bake, covered, in preheated 350F oven for about 30 minutes. Uncover and continue baking for 15 minutes longer, until noodles are tender and lasagna is hot.

Per portion: 427 calories, 19.8 g protein, 19.6 g fat, 44.8 g carbohydrates, 4.2 g dietary fibre, 266 mg calcium, 1.8 mg iron, 36 mcg folacin. Excellent source of vitamin A, vitamin C and vitamin B6. Good source of folacin, vitamin B12, calcium and zinc. High in dietary fibre.

QUICK CHILI LASAGNA

 Oven-ready noodles are a boon to the time-pressed cook. Now you can have lasagna on the table with half the mess and fuss.

Serves 8 to 10

2	700-mL jars meatless spaghetti sauce, preferably spicy
2 ½ cups	diced cooked chicken
1	19-oz can kidney or black beans, rinsed and drained
1 ½ cups	frozen corn niblets
1	onion, chopped
2	garlic cloves, minced
1 tbsp	chili powder
12 to 15	oven-ready lasagna noodles
1	200-g pkg (5 slices) mozzarella cheese
1 cup	grated cheddar cheese

1. Combine spaghetti sauce, chicken, beans, corn, onion, garlic and chili powder in a large saucepan and heat until hot. Reserve 1 ½ cups of sauce for the top.

2. Spread 1 ½ cups sauce on the bottom of a 9 x 13-inch pan. Arrange four to five uncooked lasagna noodles over the sauce, spacing them ½ inch apart. (If necessary, break noodles in half to fit.) Spread half of the remaining sauce over noodles, followed by half the mozzarella slices (they will not completely cover sauce). Repeat with another layer of noodles, sauce and mozzarella. Top with remaining noodles and reserved sauce. Make sure noodles are completely covered in sauce. Sprinkle with cheddar cheese.

3. Bake, covered, in preheated 350F oven for about 30 minutes. Uncover and continue to bake for another 15 minutes until noodles are tender and lasagna is hot.

Per portion: 463 calories, 27.5 g protein, 16 g fat, 54.6 g carbohydrates, 7.1 g dietary fibre, 257 mg calcium, 2.2 mg iron, 53 mcg folacin. Excellent source of vitamin A, vitamin B6. Good source of vitamin C, folacin and vitamin B12. High in dietary fibre.

 The lasagna will appear to be quite liquid before you bake it, but the noodles will absorb some of the sauce, and it will thicken.

PASTA AND ITALIAN SAUSAGE

MW READER RECIPE: Sally and Chris Hermansen of Vancouver rely on this pasta sausage dish all the time. "We add julienned carrots so that Carl and twins Anna and Grace don't notice them." The sauce simmers by itself, so Sally can play with the kids while dinner's on the go.

Serves 4

4	hot or sweet Italian sausages
1	large carrot, cut into thin julienne strips
1	onion, diced
2	garlic cloves, minced
2 tsp	dried basil
1	28-oz can plum tomatoes, including juice
1	450-g pkg rigatoni or penne
	Parmesan cheese (optional)

1. Remove the casings from sausages. Crumble the sausage meat into a medium-sized saucepan. Cook sausage meat, stirring frequently, until no longer pink. Drain fat, leaving sausage in saucepan. Add carrot, onion and garlic, and cook, stirring frequently, until vegetables soften slightly.

2. Add basil and tomatoes with their juice; crush tomatoes slightly. Partially cover and gently simmer for about 1 hour, stirring occasionally.

3. Cook pasta according to package directions. Drain and toss with sauce. Serve with Parmesan.

Per portion: 374 calories, 23 g protein, 11.1 g fat, 46.8 g carbohydrates, 5 g dietary fibre, 100 mg calcium, 3.3 mg iron, 26 mcg folacin. Excellent source of vitamin A. Good source of vitamin C, vitamin B6 and iron. High in dietary fibre.

Sometimes Sally adds cooked chopped bacon or pancetta to her sauce to give it a smokier flavor.

Spicy Winter
Vegetable Soup

Page 9

Spinach Salad
with Blue-Cheese
Dressing

Page 20

Colorful
Crunchy Coleslaw

Page 21

Barbecued
Vegetable and
Penne Salad

Page 24

Rice and Beans

Page 42

**Tortellini
with Bacon and
Rosemary Sauce**

Page 48

Turkey, Fennel
and Sundried
Tomato Fusilli

Page 51

Mediterranean
Tuna Penne

Page 54

Spicy Chicken and
Red Pepper Penne

Page 59

Wild
Mushroom Pasta

Page 60

Pasta and
Italian Sausage

Page 68

Simple
Poached Chicken

Page 81

Honey Chicken

Page 82

Quick Quesadillas

Page 83

Slow-Cooker
Beef Stew

Page 92

Broiled Salmon
with Roasted Red
Pepper Sauce

Page 95

EASY CHICKEN TETRAZZINI

MW READER RECIPE: Laurie Mustard is one busy woman. As well as raising her own four children, she also runs a daycare from her home. When she cooks, she turns to tasty, easy-to-prepare recipes. The bonus with Easy Chicken Tetrazzini is that it's nutritious and "even the kids love it."

Serves 4

1 tbsp	olive or vegetable oil
4	chicken legs or breasts
2	medium onions, chopped
1 large	garlic clove, minced
½ cup	tightly packed sliced mushrooms
½ cup	diced celery
10 oz	canned cream of mushroom soup
½ cup	milk
1 tbsp	chopped parsley
½ tsp	freshly ground black pepper
½	450-g pkg spaghetti, cooked
¼ cup	freshly grated Parmesan cheese

1.   Heat oil over medium heat in a large skillet. Add chicken, and brown for 5 minutes a side, or until skin is golden brown all over. Remove chicken from the pan, and set it aside. Reduce heat to medium low. Drain all but 1 tablespoon fat from the pan.

2.   Add onions, garlic, mushrooms and celery to the pan. Cook, stirring frequently and scraping up brown bits from the bottom of the pan, until onion is barely tender, about 3 minutes. Add soup, milk, parsley and pepper to the skillet and stir to combine. Return chicken, skin side up, to the pan. Increase heat to high. Bring the mixture just to the boil, cover, and reduce heat to very low and simmer gently for 20 minutes. Stir occasionally. Pour the sauce over spaghetti in a casserole dish. Arrange chicken over top. Sprinkle with cheese and bake uncovered in a preheated 400F oven for 20 to 25 minutes.

Per portion: 641 calories, 42.2 g protein, 28 g fat, 52.9 g carbohydrates, 3.4 g dietary fibre, 181 mg calcium, 3 mg iron

If you're watching your fat intake, the skin can be removed from the chicken and discarded before browning.

QUICK CHICKEN FUSILLI

 Fennel seeds and hot chili flakes can be stirred into adult portions after the kid-friendly version has been served.

Serves 3

½	450-g pkg fusilli, penne or rotini
1	hot or sweet Italian sausage
2	boneless skinless chicken breasts
2 tsp	vegetable or olive oil
1	onion, cut into thin strips
1	red pepper, cut into thin strips
1	green pepper, cut into thin strips
6	mushrooms, sliced
½ cup	tomato juice or tomato cocktail
½ tsp	Italian seasoning
¼ tsp	fennel seed (optional)
	Pinch of hot chili flakes
	Salt and pepper to taste
	Parmesan cheese

1. Cook pasta in a large pot of boiling salted water, stirring occasionally just until tender. Drain well.
2. Meanwhile, cut sausage into ½-inch slices and cut chicken into ¾-inch chunks. Heat oil in a large frying pan over medium heat. Add sausage to the pan and cook for 2 minutes. Add chicken and cook, stirring frequently, until sausage and chicken are cooked through — about 5 minutes.
3. Add onion, green and red peppers and mushrooms to the pan. Cook, stirring frequently, until tender. Add tomato juice to the pan along with all seasonings except salt and pepper. Cover, reduce heat to low, and simmer gently for 5 minutes until flavors blend. Taste, then add salt and pepper. Toss with hot pasta and serve with Parmesan cheese.

Per serving: 518 calories, 33.7 g protein, 12.2 g fat, 67.6 g carbohydrates, 6 g dietary fibre, 51 mg calcium, 3.1 mg iron. Excellent source of vitamin C, niacin, magnesium and zinc. Good source of iron. Very high in dietary fibre.

SKILLET CHEESY TUNA AND PENNE TOSS

 Here's a tasty dinner you can have on the table in less than half an hour.

Serves 2

½	450-g pkg penne
1 tbsp	olive oil
1	carrot, thinly sliced
1	small red pepper, finely chopped
2	garlic cloves, minced
1 large	tomato, cored and chopped
1	6.5-oz can tuna, drained
¼ cup	finely chopped fresh basil or parsley
1 cup	grated cheddar cheese, preferably old
	Salt and pepper to taste

1. Bring a large pot of salted water to a boil. Add penne and cook for 8 to 10 minutes until tender. Drain well.
2. Meanwhile, heat oil in a frying pan over medium heat. Add carrot, red pepper and garlic and cook, stirring occasionally, until barely tender. Add tomato and continue to cook for about 5 minutes until tomato has softened and juices are released. Remove from heat.
3. Stir in pasta, tuna, basil, cheese, salt and pepper. Serve immediately.

Per serving: 603 calories, 34.7 g protein, 22.7 g fat, 64 g carbohydrates, 5.1 g dietary fibre, 315 mg calcium, 3 mg iron. Excellent source of vitamin C and calcium. High in dietary fibre. Good source of iron.

CHICKEN NOODLE STIR FRY

power PICK Chow mein noodles can be found in most supermarkets. If you can't find them, cook 1 ½ cups broken dried spaghetti, and add to the stir fry.

Serves 4 to 6

½ cup	chicken, vegetable or beef broth
3 tbsp	oyster sauce
2 tbsp	soy sauce
½ tsp	dark sesame oil
1	350-g pkg steamed fresh chow mein noodles
1 tbsp	vegetable oil
1 small	onion, thinly sliced into strips
2	garlic cloves, minced
2 tsp	minced ginger
2	boneless skinless chicken breasts, cut into thin bite-sized strips
1	carrot, cut into thin bite-sized strips
1	red pepper, cut into thin bite-sized strips
3 cups	shredded Chinese nappa or green cabbage
2	green onions, thinly sliced

1. Stir together broth, oyster sauce, soy sauce and sesame oil until blended. Cook noodles according to package directions; drain well and set aside. In a very large frying pan or wok, heat oil over medium-high heat. Add onion, garlic and ginger; cook, stirring continuously, until onion has softened slightly. Add chicken and carrot. Continue to cook until carrot has softened and chicken is cooked. If the mixture sticks at all, add a bit of chicken broth or water.
2. Add noodles, red pepper, cabbage and oyster sauce mixture. Continue to stir until heated through. Stir in green onions. Serve immediately.

Per portion: 407 calories, 26.4 g protein, 7.2 g fat, 59.1 g carbohydrates, 6.6 g dietary fibre, 89 mg calcium, 2.5 mg iron, 65 mcg folacin. Excellent source of vitamin A and vitamin B6. Good source of vitamin B12, iron and zinc. Very high in dietary fibre.

MID-WEEK MAIN COURSES

If you're like us, you're always on the lookout for quick dinner ideas that taste good but don't take hours to prepare. That's why *Modern Woman's* Food Editor, Heather Trim, creates food pages that offer everyday recipes for weekday meals. "I think food should be simple to prepare and good to eat," explains our cooking dynamo. "That's the only way I cook! So our basic recipes use easy-to-find ingredients and the directions are straightforward."

Menu planning made easy — that's the idea behind these mid-week main courses. Still, easy doesn't have to mean dull — these tempting recipes come from many different cultures. You can choose a traditional Perfect Roasted Chicken or you can jazz up your table with a Caribbean Chicken Pie. From Peppercorn and Mustard Steak to savory Greek-Style Meatballs, there is a variety of fun and festive dishes to lift mealtime up out of the ordinary.

PERFECT ROASTED CHICKEN

What could be better than roasted chicken for dinner? Crispy golden-brown skin, juicy flavorful meat. And a bonus: minimal effort for the cook.

Serves 4

3 ½-lb	whole chicken
	Salt and freshly ground black pepper
1 tbsp	butter, at room temperature

1.   Preheat oven to 400F. Remove giblets and neck from the cavity of the chicken, along with any excess fat. Sprinkle the cavity with salt and pepper. Rub the outside of chicken with butter, then sprinkle with salt and pepper.
2.   Place chicken on its side on a rack set in a small roasting pan. Roast chicken for 20 minutes, then baste. Turn chicken to the other side, roast for 20 minutes more, then baste. Turn chicken breast side up and continue to roast for 30 to 35 minutes, basting occasionally. Chicken is ready when juices run clear when a knife is inserted into a thigh, or a thermometer placed in the thigh registers 185F.
3.   Let chicken stand for 10 minutes before carving.

Per portion: 417 calories, 47.7 g protein, 23.8 g fat, 0 g carbohydrates, 0 g dietary fibre, 26 mg calcium, 2.2 mg iron. Good source of iron.

For even browning, the chicken should be turned while roasting, but you can skip this by putting the seasoned chicken on a rack, breast side up, and roasting for about 1 1/4 hours, basting frequently.

ROSEMARY DIJON CHICKEN

Low sodium chicken broth is recommended because regular chicken broth will become too salty as the sauce boils down and concentrates.

Serves 4

1 tbsp	olive or vegetable oil
4	boneless, skinless chicken breasts
⅓ cup	finely chopped onion
2	garlic cloves, minced
½ tsp	rosemary leaves, crumbled
½ cup	chicken broth, preferably low sodium
1 ½ tbsp	Dijon mustard

¼ cup   whipping cream
             Salt and black pepper to taste

1.   Heat oil in a large frying pan over medium heat. Add chicken and cook for 4 to 5 minutes per side, or until chicken is cooked through. Remove chicken to a plate and cover loosely with foil to keep warm.
2.   Add onion, garlic and rosemary to the pan (if necessary, add a bit more oil) and cook for 1 minute. Add chicken broth, stirring to scrape up any brown bits from the bottom of the pan. Whisk in Dijon and whipping cream. Bring the mixture to a boil and cook through until it thickens to a sauce-like consistency. Add salt and pepper to taste. Return chicken breasts to pan to warm, then serve.

Per serving: 329 calories, 18 g protein, 21.2 g fat, 16.2 g carbohydrates, 0.8 g dietary fibre, 238 mg calcium, 1.6 mg iron.

CHICKEN, BROCCOLI AND SALSA QUICHE

Use a store-purchased pie shell, and this quiche will be on the table in no time. Feel free to substitute mushrooms or peppers for broccoli.

Serves 6

1 cup	cooked chicken (½-inch diced)
½ cup	coarsely chopped cooked broccoli
1 ¼ cups	grated Monterey Jack or cheddar cheese
1	green onion, thinly sliced
1	9-inch pie shell, partially baked
¾ cup	milk
2	eggs, lightly beaten
2 tbsp	salsa
	Generous pinches of salt and black pepper to taste

1.   Preheat oven to 350F. Scatter chicken, broccoli, cheese and green onion over the base of the pie shell. Place the pie shell on a cookie sheet. Whisk together milk, eggs, salsa, salt and pepper until blended. Pour over the chicken mixture.
2.   Bake for 40 to 45 minutes, or just until quiche is set. Do not overbake or eggs will be tough. Let stand for 10 minutes before serving.

Per serving: 223 calories, 28.2 g protein, 10.5 g fat, 2.8 g carbohydrates, 0.2 g dietary fibre, 37 mg calcium, 1.1 mg iron. Good source of calcium.

CARIBBEAN CHICKEN PIE

Jump up and celebrate with this great-tasting pie.

Serves 8

1 tbsp	vegetable oil
1 ½ lb	ground chicken
3	garlic cloves, minced
1 tsp each	allspice, cinnamon, nutmeg and chili flakes
1 ½ cups	chicken broth
1 ½ cups	peeled and diced sweet potato (about ⅓-inch pieces)
1	19-oz can black beans, rinsed and drained
¾ cup	dried bread crumbs
1 cup	chopped green onions (about 5)
½ cup	chopped parsley
½ tsp	salt
2	frozen 9-inch deep-dish pie shells

1. In a large skillet, heat oil over medium-high heat. Add ground chicken, garlic, allspice, cinnamon, nutmeg and chili flakes. Cook, stirring, until chicken is no longer pink. Add broth and bring to a boil. Add sweet potato. Reduce heat and simmer for 8 to 10 minutes. Remove from heat. Stir in black beans, bread crumbs, green onions, parsley and salt. Cool.

2. Preheat oven to 375F. Partially thaw pie shells. Place one shell on a cookie sheet and spoon in filling. Cover with second pie shell. Crimp edges to seal. Cut three (1-inch) steam vents in the top pastry. Bake for 50 to 60 minutes until pastry is golden. Let stand for 10 minutes before slicing.

Per portion: 520 calories, 23.6 g protein, 25.2 g fat, 49.5 g carbohydrates, 5.2 g dietary fibre, 64 mg calcium, 4 mg iron

To freeze the pie, wrap it in waxed paper, then in foil. To bake after freezing, let the pie stand at room temperature for 1 hour. Bake at 375F for 1 hour. Cover with foil and continue to bake for 30 minutes. If pastry is a little damp, uncover and bake 10 more minutes.

PAD THAI

(Thai fried rice noodles)

MW READER RECIPE: Merla McMenomy is the co-owner of The Art of Food cooking school in Toronto. Merla's popular Pad Thai recipe is from her Thai cooking class.

Serves 4 to 6

½ lb	dried flat rice noodles
½ cup	unsalted dry-roasted peanuts
⅓ cup	fish sauce (nam pla)
3 tbsp	brown sugar
¼ cup	ketchup
2 tbsp	white vinegar
¼ cup	vegetable oil
½ lb	boneless pork loin, cut into small pieces
½ lb	medium shrimp, shelled and deveined
1 tbsp	minced garlic
3	eggs, lightly beaten
4 ½ cups	bean sprouts
4	green onions, cut into 1-inch lengths
¼ cup	finely chopped coriander
	Coriander sprigs and lime wedges

1. Put noodles in a large bowl and cover them with lukewarm water; let stand to soften — about 1 hour. Drain and set aside. Meanwhile, toast nuts in an ungreased skillet over medium-low heat for 5 minutes, stirring frequently. Coarsely chop them and set aside. Combine fish sauce, sugar, ketchup and vinegar in a bowl.

2. Heat wok over high heat. Add oil and swirl to coat the bottom of the pan. Add pork; stir-fry for 2 minutes. Add shrimp and garlic; stir-fry for 1 minute. Push the contents of the pan to one side. Add eggs in the centre of the pan and scramble, about 30 seconds. Stir in the fish sauce mixture and bring to a boil. Add noodles and toss. Stir in 4 cups bean sprouts, ⅓ cup peanuts, green onions and chopped coriander; toss until hot. Transfer to serving platter, sprinkle with remaining peanuts and garnish with remaining bean sprouts, coriander and lime wedges.

Per portion: 727 calories, 39.3 g protein, 31.5 g fat, 74.7 g carbohydrates, 4.2 g dietary fibre, 120 mg calcium, 4.7 mg iron. Excellent source of iron.

MEE GORENG

(Fried noodles Indian style)

quick & EASY This tasty, healthy recipe from the Singapore Tourist Promotion Board has been adapted for *MW* readers.

Serves 3 to 4

8 oz	fresh Chinese egg noodles
2 tbsp	ketchup
2 tsp	hot red chili sauce
1 tsp	granulated sugar
½ tsp	salt
2 tbsp	vegetable oil
2 large	garlic cloves, minced
1 tsp	hot green pepper, finely chopped
1	boneless, skinless chicken breast cut into small pieces
1 ½ cups	Chinese cabbage, coarsely chopped
1	tomato, chopped
1-inch piece	deep-fried tofu, cut into thin strips
1 medium	potato, cooked, peeled and diced
2	eggs, lightly beaten
3 cups	bean sprouts
	Sliced hot green chili peppers, fried red onion and lemon wedges

1. Bring a large pot of salted water to a boil. Add noodles, bring back to a boil and cook for 1 minute. Drain, rinse in cold water and shake off any excess water. Stir ketchup with chili sauce, sugar and salt.
2. Heat oil in a wok over medium heat. Add garlic and hot green pepper; cook, stirring constantly. When garlic is golden brown, increase the heat to high and add chicken, cabbage, tomato, tofu and potato. Stir-fry until vegetables are tender, for 30 to 60 seconds. Add noodles and ketchup mixture, tossing. Push contents to the side of the pan; add eggs and stir to scramble just until they begin to set. Add bean sprouts; toss until eggs are cooked and sprouts are wilted. Transfer to a platter. Sprinkle with sliced chili peppers, fried red onion and a squeeze of lemon juice. Serve immediately.

Per portion: 503 calories, 27.8 g protein, 15.4 g fat, 66 g carbohydrates, 7.1 g dietary fibre, 110 mg calcium, 3.6 mg iron. Excellent source of dietary fibre, iron and vitamin C.

SPEEDY MOROCCAN-STYLE CHICKEN

MW READER RECIPE: Readers Brenda Menezes and David Royle con-
tributed this recipe as a quick mealtime strategy for working moms and
dads. Brenda grew up eating spicy foods, so she and David are both keen
to introduce their boys, Christopher and Patrick, to new spices and tastes.
The kids don't seem to mind a bit!

Serves 4

1 ½ tbsp	olive oil
4	boneless, skinless chicken breasts
½ cup	finely chopped onion
2	garlic cloves, minced
1 tsp	minced fresh ginger
1 tsp each	ground cumin and paprika
½ tsp each	ground cinnamon and turmeric
½ cup	undiluted canned chicken broth
2 tbsp	lemon juice
⅓ cup	pitted black olives or pimento-stuffed green olives
1 tbsp	finely chopped fresh coriander (optional)
	Freshly ground black pepper

1. In a large wide saucepan, heat oil over medium-high heat. Add chicken,
onion, garlic, ginger, cumin, paprika, cinnamon and turmeric. Cook for 3 to 5
minutes or just until chicken is no longer pink on the outside and onion is softened slightly. The chicken will not be thoroughly cooked.
2. Add chicken broth and lemon juice. Cover and bring to a boil, then reduce
heat to simmer. Add olives and coriander, if using. Cover and continue to cook
for 2 to 3 more minutes, just until chicken is cooked through. Serve chicken
and sauce over couscous or rice. Sprinkle with black pepper. Nice topped with
cooked carrots or green beans.

Per portion: 210 calories, 28.6 g protein, 8.2 g fat, 4.7 g carbohydrates,
1 g dietary fibre, 43 mg calcium, 2.1 mg iron

Growing kids are little eating machines, snacking their way from breakfast to
lunch, lunch to dinner and dinner to bedtime. To fill those bottomless pits
with a healthy snack, take your cue from Brenda: she keeps packaged noo-
dle soups on hand and throws in leftover vegetables for extra nutrition.

CHICKEN PELAU

Here's a dish to serve during Caribana, Toronto's largest summer festival. In the weeks leading up to the spectacular carnival parade, Toronto comes alive with traditional cultural events such as calypso, steel band, folk dance and traditional drumming.

Serves 6

3 ½ lb	chicken
4 large	garlic cloves, minced
1 ½-inch	chunk ginger, peeled and finely chopped
	Salt and freshly ground black pepper
4 oz	salted beef, cut into ¼-inch pieces (optional)
2 tbsp	vegetable oil
1 tbsp	butter
1 small	Spanish onion, finely chopped
1 large	tomato, chopped
1	14-oz can pigeon peas, well drained
½	7-oz pkg pure creamed coconut, chopped
3 tbsp	soy sauce
3 large	sprigs fresh thyme
1	hot pepper, preferably scotch bonnet
2 cups	long-grain white rice
4 cups	water

1. Cut chicken into 8 pieces; remove the skin and discard. (It is difficult to remove skin from the wings. Leave it on if you wish.) Place chicken wings in a shallow dish. In a small bowl, stir garlic with ginger and ½ teaspoon each of salt and pepper. Using your hands, rub the mixture into chicken pieces until evenly coated. Leave at room temperature for 30 minutes.

2. If using salted beef, place it in a small saucepan. Cover with cold water, then bring to a boil. Once the water boils, drain, then cover beef again with cold water and bring to a boil. Drain water and set beef aside (this helps remove salt from beef).

3. When chicken has finished marinating, heat oil and butter over medium high in a large, wide, deep saucepan or skillet. Add chicken pieces and cook for 7 to 8 minutes, turning them frequently, scraping ginger and garlic from the bottom of the pan. Chicken should be golden brown. Do not crowd the pan. If necessary, cook in two batches. Add onion and tomato and cook for 3 to 4 minutes, stirring occasionally to soften onion slightly.

4.   Stir in pigeon peas, creamed coconut, soy sauce, thyme, whole pepper, salted beef, rice and water. Bring to a boil, stirring occasionally to help dissolve creamed coconut. Cover, reduce heat to low and simmer gently for 30 minutes. Taste and add more salt and pepper if you wish. Remove scotch bonnet pepper and thyme before serving.

Per portion: 586 calories, 36.7 g protein, 18.4 g fat, 67.4 g carbohydrates, 4.9 g dietary fibre, 74 mg calcium, 3.1 mg iron

 All the ingredients can be purchased in West Indian food stores. Most are also available in your supermarket, and some of them, such as ginger, soy sauce and creamed coconut, can be found in Asian supermarkets.

SIMPLE POACHED CHICKEN

 Serve a dollop of these easy mayonnaise mixtures with poached chicken: mayonnaise mixed with mango chutney and cayenne pepper to taste; or mayonnaise mixed with minced jalapeño pepper and chopped coriander to taste.

Serves 2

1	cup water
½ cup	white wine (optional)
1 medium	onion, cut into thick wedges
1 small	carrot, cut into thick slices
2	bay leaves
2	garlic cloves, minced
2	black peppercorns
2	sprigs fresh parsley or thyme
2	boneless, skinless chicken breasts

1.   Put all the ingredients in a large frying pan or wide saucepan. Cover, and slowly bring to a simmer over medium heat. Gently simmer chicken for about 10 minutes, until the chicken is just cooked and no longer pink inside. Remove with a slotted spoon. Use poached chicken in chicken salads, casseroles or sandwiches. The poaching liquid can be frozen and used to make soups.

Per serving: 128 calories, 26.7 g protein, 1.5 g fat, 0 g carbohydrates, 0 g dietary fibre, 13 mg calcium, 0.9 mg iron, 3 mcg folacin. Excellent source of vitamin B6. Good source of vitamin B12.

CHILI PEPPER CHICKEN

weight SMART *MW* READER RECIPE: Shelley Rae, freelance writer and small business owner, knows what it's like when the clock strikes six.

Serves 4

4	chicken breasts, legs or thighs, skin removed
3 tbsp	soy sauce
1 tbsp	sesame oil
1 tbsp	lemon juice
½ tsp	hot chili flakes
½ tsp	seasoned or black pepper

1. Preheat oven to 400F. Place chicken pieces, meat side down, in a baking dish just large enough to hold them. In a small bowl, whisk together soy sauce, sesame oil, lemon juice, hot chili flakes and pepper. Pour it over chicken and turn to coat.
2. Bake chicken for 35 to 45 minutes. Baste chicken occasionally, and turn once, halfway through cooking. When cooked, spoon off the excess fat and use the remaining juice as gravy. Serve with rice and broccoli.

Per portion: 168 calories, 27.9 g protein, 4.9 g fat, 1.5 g carbohydrates, 0.1 g dietary fibre, 17 mg calcium, 1.2 mg iron, 5 mcg folacin. Excellent source of vitamin B6. Good source of vitamin B12.

HONEY CHICKEN

To produce 1 pound (500 g) of honey, a bee would have to travel the earth's orbit three times.

Serves 4

1 tbsp	olive or vegetable oil
4	boneless, skinless chicken breasts
	Salt and freshly ground black pepper
⅓ cup	chicken broth, preferably low-salt
2 tbsp	red wine vinegar
2 tbsp	honey
2 tsp	Dijon mustard

1.   Heat oil in a large wide frying pan over medium heat. Sprinkle both sides of chicken with salt and pepper. Put chicken in the frying pan and cook it for 4 to 5 minutes per side, until cooked through. Remove it to a plate and cover it loosely to keep it warm.

2.   Add broth, vinegar, honey and Dijon to the saucepan. Increase heat to high, and stir to scrape any brown bits from the pan. Boil until thickened slightly and deep brown in color. Pour over chicken and serve immediately.

Per portion: 196 calories, 26.7 g protein, 5 g fat, 9.3 g carbohydrates, 0 g dietary fibre, 17 mg calcium, 1 mg iron. Excellent source of vitamin B6 and good source of vitamin B12.

QUICK QUESADILLAS

Mark hot quesadillas "handle with care" by garnishing them with additional jalapeño rings on top.

Serves 4

4 oz	crumbled goat's cheese (about ⅔ cup)
1 cup	grated cheddar cheese
1	jalapeño pepper, seeded and minced
½ cup	chopped coriander
4	green onions, finely chopped
4	10-inch flour tortillas
½ lb	thinly sliced ham or cooked chicken, cut into strips (about 2 cups)
¼ cup	salsa

1.   Preheat oven to 450F. In a small bowl, stir together goat's cheese, cheddar cheese, jalapeño pepper, coriander and green onions until combined.

2.   Lightly brush tortillas with water. Layer ham and cheese filling on one-half of each tortilla. Dot with salsa. Fold tortilla over to cover the filling and form a semicircle. Place the filled tortillas in 2 lightly greased baking dishes so they are not touching.

3.   Bake, uncovered, until hot — 5 to 6 minutes. Cut each in half. For crisper quesadillas, heat about 1 teaspoon vegetable oil in a large frying pan over medium heat. Fry the quesadillas in batches, 2 to 3 minutes per side, until crisp and brown. Cut each in half and serve.

Per portion: 475 calories, 28.9 g protein, 23.4 g fat, 36.9 g carbohydrates, 1.8 g dietary fibre, 456 mg calcium, 3.7 mg iron. Excellent source of calcium and iron.

CHICKEN PATICHKI

MW READER RECIPE: Nadia Andrushko cooked for five years at the Ukrainian pavilion during Caravan, Toronto's annual multicultural celebration, and now, 20 years later, she has a second career, catering for hundreds at Ukrainian weddings and other special occasions. Nadia tries hard to use recipes that are low in fat, but in the case of the patichki, frying adds flavor, so why change a good recipe?

Makes about 14 skewers

1 ½ lbs	boneless skinless chicken breasts
1 small	onion, quartered
1	garlic clove
1 tsp	salt
½ tsp	black pepper
1	egg, lightly beaten
1 tbsp	water
1 cup	dried bread crumbs
	Vegetable oil for frying
2	celery stalks, coarsely chopped
2 medium	carrots, coarsely chopped
1	onion, coarsely chopped

1. Cut chicken into 1-inch cubes; set aside in a medium-sized bowl. Purée onion and garlic in a food processor until fairly smooth. Remove and toss with chicken, salt and pepper. Cover and refrigerate at least 2 and up to 6 hours. Using small bamboo skewers (about 4 inches long), tightly thread chicken onto the skewers.
2. Whisk egg with water in a shallow dish. Put bread crumbs in another shallow dish. Dip chicken in egg, then roll in bread crumbs; set aside on waxed paper; repeat with remaining skewers. Pour oil in a large deep skillet (oil should be about 1 inch deep) and heat over medium-high heat until it reaches 375F on a deep-fry thermometer. Add a few chicken skewers at a time and cook just until outside is deep golden brown, about 45 seconds per side (if chicken darkens too quickly, the oil is too hot). Chicken should not be cooked inside.
3. Preheat oven to 375F. Put celery, carrots and onion on the bottom of a medium-sized shallow casserole dish. Prop chicken skewers up as best you can against the side of the casserole, then cover the dish. Bake for 15 minutes. Reduce oven to 350F and continue to bake for 45 minutes. Serve with rice pilaf and a tossed green salad.

Per skewer: 90 calories, 12 g protein, 2.4 g fat, 4.4 g carbohydrates,
0.2 g dietary fibre, 15 mg calcium, 0.6 mg iron

 Nadia uses wooden skewers made especially for patichki that are available in Ukrainian stores. However, bamboo skewers cut into 4-inch lengths work well too.

FAMILY BBQ WINGS

Serve these wings with the Savory Salsa Potatoes featured on page 31.

Makes 36 wings

2 lb	whole chicken wings (about 18 wings)
1 tbsp	vegetable oil
½ cup	finely chopped onion
2	garlic cloves, minced
¾ cup	chili sauce
1 tbsp	Worcestershire sauce
2 tsp	Tabasco

1. Cut wing tips from chicken wings (discard the tips or save them for chicken stock). Cut wings in half at the joint.
2. Preheat broiler. Set a rack on a foil-lined baking sheet or broiler pan. Place wings on the rack, spacing them about ½ inch apart. Broil them under the preheated broiler, about 3 inches from heating element, for 8 to 10 minutes or until golden brown and the skin is crisp. Turn and continue to broil for 8 to 10 more minutes until golden brown and chicken is cooked.
3. Meanwhile, heat oil in a medium saucepan over medium heat. Add onion and garlic, and cook for 5 minutes or until soft. Stir in chili sauce, Worcestershire sauce and Tabasco. Bring to a boil, then reduce heat and simmer, uncovered, for 5 minutes to allow flavors to blend. Turn mixture into a large bowl.
4. Once wings are cooked, remove them from the oven and put them in the bowl with the chili sauce mixture. Toss to coat well. Return to rack, broil for 1 minute, turn, brush with any remaining barbecue sauce, and broil for 1 minute.

Per piece: 35 calories, 2.5 g protein, 2 g fat, 1.7 g carbohydrates,
0.4 g dietary fibre, 0.3 mg calcium, 0.2 mg iron

 No time to make the sauce? Just add a dash of Worcestershire sauce and Tabasco to your favourite bottle of BBQ sauce.

CHICKEN FINGERS AND
HONEY YOGURT DIPPING SAUCE

Kids love chicken fingers! Serve your own homemade variety for a crowd-pleasing treat.

Makes 16

2 tbsp	dried bread crumbs
1 tsp each	basil and oregano
½ tsp	thyme
¼ tsp each	garlic salt, onion powder, paprika and salt
	Ground black pepper
2	boneless skinless chicken breasts

Dipping Sauce

2 tbsp	plain yogurt
2 tsp	liquid honey
1 tsp	mayonnaise
¼ tsp	Dijon mustard
	Salt and pepper to taste

1.   Preheat oven to 400F. Put bread crumbs, basil, oregano, thyme, garlic salt, onion powder, paprika and salt and pepper in a sturdy clear plastic bag. Shake to combine.

2.   Cut chicken into strips about ½ inch wide, then cut into 2-inch-long pieces. Rinse them under cold water; shake off excess water. Put a few strips at a time into the bag, shaking until coated. Place them on a lightly greased baking sheet. Repeat with remaining chicken pieces. Bake for about 15 minutes, turning halfway through cooking.

3.   Meanwhile, prepare the sauce by stirring all the ingredients together in a small bowl. Serve hot chicken fingers with dipping sauce on the side.

Per chicken finger: 26 calories, 3.6 g protein, 0.5 g fat, 1.6 g carbohydrates, 9 mg calcium, 0.2 mg iron

RED WINE AND HERB MARINATED LAMB KEBABS

Welcome summer by firing up the barbecue and serving easy-to-prepare kebabs the whole family will enjoy.

Serves 8

3 lb	boneless leg of lamb (thawed if frozen)
½ cup	dry red wine
¼ cup	olive oil
6	garlic cloves, minced
⅓ cup	finely chopped mixed fresh herbs such as parsley, rosemary, thyme, oregano or 1 ½ tbsp dried mixed herbs
½ tsp	freshly ground black pepper
½ tsp	salt
1	seedless orange, sliced and quartered

1. Trim away excess fat from the outside of lamb. Cut lamb into 1-inch cubes. Whisk the remaining ingredients — except orange — together in a large bowl. Add lamb and toss until well combined. Cover (or transfer to a sturdy resealable plastic bag), and refrigerate overnight, or at least 4 hours, stirring occasionally to make sure lamb is well coated in marinade.
2. Just before skewering the kebabs, toss them with salt. Skewer beginning with lamb pieces and alternating occasionally with the orange sections. Barbecue on a medium-high grill for 7 to 9 minutes, turning occasionally until lamb is pink inside.

Per serving: 244 calories, 29.6 g protein, 11.6 g fat, 3.2 g carbohydrates, 0.4 g dietary fibre, 26 mg calcium, 2.8 mg iron

If you don't have time to cube the meat, marinate the whole boneless leg overnight, then barbecue the roast for about 15 minutes per side for medium-rare. Beef is a tasty substitute for lamb.

HONOLULU PORK KEBABS

This recipe works just as well with cubed boneless chicken breasts.

Serves 6

2	pork tenderloins (¾ lb)
⅓ cup	teriyaki sauce
¼ cup	peanut or vegetable oil
2 tbsp	brown sugar
1 tbsp	Dijon mustard
1 tbsp	finely minced ginger
1 tbsp	minced garlic cloves
½ tsp	cayenne pepper
1 ½ cups	fresh or canned pineapple chunks (14-oz can)

1. Cut pork tenderloin into 1-inch cubes and set aside in a large bowl or a sturdy resealable plastic bag.
2. Whisk the remaining ingredients (except pineapple chunks) together. Pour over pork and stir to ensure it is evenly coated in marinade. Cover and refrigerate overnight, or at least 4 hours.
3. Skewer pork, alternating occasionally with a chunk of pineapple. Barbecue on medium-high grill for about 8 minutes, turning occasionally, until pork is cooked through.

Per serving: 178 calories, 18.6 g protein, 7.9 g fat, 7.8 g carbohydrates, 0.4 g dietary fibre, 15 mg calcium, 1.3 mg iron

PEPPERCORN AND MUSTARD STEAK

 These steaks are unbeatable when you serve them smothered in sautéed mushrooms and onions.

Serves 2 generously

¼ cup	dried bread crumbs
3 tbsp	Dijon Mustard
2 tbsp	finely chopped parsley
	Generous pinch of salt and black pepper
2	6-oz eye-of-round steaks
1 to 2 tbsp	vegetable or olive oil

| 8 | mushrooms, cut in half |
| 1 small | red or cooking onion, thinly sliced |

1. Put bread crumbs in a small, shallow dish. In a small bowl, stir Dijon with parsley, salt and pepper until blended. Spread the mustard mixture over steaks. Coat steaks with bread crumbs, pressing firmly to help crumbs adhere. Set aside on waxed paper.
2. Heat 1 tablespoon of oil in a frying pan over medium heat. Add steaks and cook for 3 to 5 minutes. Turn carefully and cook for another 3 minutes for medium-rare. Remove steaks from the pan and cover loosely to keep warm.
3. Increase heat to medium high. Add mushrooms and onion to the pan (adding remaining oil if necessary). Cook, stirring frequently, until soft — about 5 minutes.

Per serving: 412 calories, 42.8 g protein, 18.1 g fat, 18.8 g carbohydrates, 2.2 g dietary fibre, 73 mg calcium, 6 mg iron. Excellent source of iron. Moderate in dietary fibre.

SAGE SCALLOPINI WITH WHITE WINE

quick &
EASY   If you don't have white wine, substitute ⅓ cup apple juice.

Serves 2

1 tbsp	butter or olive oil
6	fresh sage leaves (or 1 tsp dried sage)
½ lb	pork or veal scallopini
	Salt and black pepper
⅓ cup	white wine
1 tbsp	capers (optional)

1. Heat butter over medium-high heat. Add sage leaves and cook until wilted and fragrant — about 30 to 45 seconds. Or add dried sage and cook for 45 seconds.
2. Sprinkle both sides of pork or veal with salt and pepper. Add the meat to the pan and cook until deep golden brown on both sides, about 1 minute per side. Remove to a plate and cover loosely to keep warm.
3. Increase heat and add wine to the pan, stirring to scrape up any brown bits. Add capers and cook for 1 to 2 minutes until liquid is slightly reduced. Pour wine sauce over the meat and serve immediately.

Per serving: 208 calories, 24.9 g protein, 9 g fat, 0.5 g carbohydrates, .0 g dietary fibre, 17 mg calcium, 1 mg iron. Excellent source of vitamin B.

AUTUMN SKILLET PORK

Sweet fruit and a dash of spicy Dijon give this dish a refreshing taste on a bright fall day.

Serves 4

4	centre-cut pork chops
1 tbsp	vegetable oil
	Salt, freshly ground black pepper and paprika
1 cup	apple juice or apple cider
1 tsp	Dijon mustard
½ tsp	Worcestershire sauce
1 cup	mixed dried fruit such as apricots, pitted prunes and dried apples
½ tsp	cornstarch
1 tbsp	water

1.   Trim fat from the outside edges of chops. Heat oil in a large frying pan over medium-high heat. Lightly sprinkle both sides of chops with salt, pepper and paprika. Cook until golden brown on both sides, about 3 minutes per side. Transfer chops to a plate.

2.   Add apple juice to the pan, scraping up any brown bits from the bottom. Whisk in Dijon and Worcestershire sauce. Return chops and any juices that have accumulated to the pan; cover, and simmer gently for 30 minutes. Turn chops and stir in dried fruit. Continue to simmer, covered, for 10 minutes, or until pork and fruit are tender.

3.   Remove pork to a platter. Using a slotted spoon, remove fruit from the pan and place them on pork. Stir cornstarch into water until dissolved. Add the cornstarch mixture into the liquid in the pan, stirring continuously until the sauce is boiling and has thickened slightly. Pour it over pork and fruit.

Per portion: 389 calories, 28.2 g protein, 10.8 g fat, 47.6 g carbohydrates, 5 g dietary fibre, 57 mg calcium, 3.4 mg iron. Good source of vitamin C and iron. High in dietary fibre.

MOM'S MEAT LOAF

We've combined three types of meat to add flavor to our meat loaf, but ground beef by itself works just fine. For a spicier meat loaf, substitute some finely chopped hot Italian sausage for the pork, then add finely chopped jalapeño pepper, Tabasco or chili flakes.

Serves 8

1	300-g pkg frozen chopped spinach, thawed
4 slices	whole wheat or white bread
⅔ cup	milk
1 lb	lean ground beef
½ lb	ground veal
½ lb	ground pork
1	medium onion, finely chopped
2	garlic cloves, minced
½ cup	freshly grated Parmesan cheese
1	egg
2 tbsp	Worcestershire sauce
1 tbsp	basil
1 tsp	salt
1 tsp	thyme
	Generous grinding of black pepper

1. Preheat oven to 350F. Using your hands, squeeze out as much liquid from spinach as possible. Cut bread into ½-inch cubes and put them in a small bowl. Add milk to bread and stir to moisten. Let it soak until ready to use — the bread should be very mushy.

2. In a large bowl, using your hands, combine ground beef with veal, pork, onion, garlic, Parmesan, egg, Worcestershire sauce, basil, salt, thyme and black pepper until barely mixed. Add spinach and soaked bread. Mix just until well combined.

3. Pat mixture into a 9 x 5 x 3-inch loaf pan, rounding the top slightly. Bake for 1 ¼ to 1 ½ hours, until meat loaf juices run clear. Drain off fat halfway through cooking and at end of cooking. Let meat loaf stand for 10 minutes before slicing.

Per serving: 290 calories, 28 g protein, 14.5 g fat, 11.5 g carbohydrates, 1.9 g dietary fibre, 184 mg calcium, 2.8 mg iron

SLOW-COOKER BEEF STEW

 MW READER RECIPE: Citytv field cameraman Patrick Pidgeon likes to prepare dinner before he leaves for work. It's a good thing too — with three children, it's nice to come home to a ready-to-eat dinner.

Serves 6 to 8

¼ cup	all-purpose flour
½ tsp each	salt and pepper
2 lbs	stewing beef, cut into 1-inch cubes
1 tbsp	olive oil
1 ½	cups beef broth
2 medium	onions, chopped
2	garlic cloves, minced
1 tsp	paprika
1 tsp	Worcestershire sauce
½ tsp	dried basil
	Generous grinding of black pepper
4 medium	carrots, cut into chunks
4 medium	potatoes, peeled and cut into chunks

1. Put flour, salt and pepper in a sealable plastic bag or in a large bowl. Add beef and shake in the bag or toss in the bowl to cover with mixture. Remove beef, shaking off the excess flour. Heat oil in a large frying pan; add meat in batches (do not crowd pan) and cook until browned. Add beef broth to the pan and stir, scraping up brown bits from the bottom of the pan.
2. Put the meat, broth and remaining ingredients in a slow cooker; stir well. Cover and turn slow cooker to low. Cook for 10 to 12 hours, until meat is tender. Or turn cooker to high and cook for 4 to 6 hours until meat is tender.

Per serving: 299 calories, 28.1 g protein, 10.1 g fat, 23 g carbohydrates, 2.5 g dietary fibre, 38 mg calcium, 3.2 mg iron, 23 mcg folacin. Excellent source of vitamin A, vitamin B6 and vitamin B12. Good source of iron. Moderate in dietary fibre.

 If you're really in a hurry, skip Step 1 and add all ingredients to a slow cooker.

GREEK-STYLE MEATBALLS

Serve room-temperature meatballs as an appetizer with tzatziki (a yogurt garlic dip, available in supermarkets), or serve warm over rice.

Makes 18

1 lb	ground veal
¼ lb	ground pork
1	egg, lightly beaten
2 tbsp	dried bread crumbs
	Juice of ½ lemon
⅓ cup	finely chopped fresh mint
1 tsp	dried oregano
¾ tsp	salt
	Fresh ground black pepper
	About 1 tbsp olive oil for frying

1. In a medium-sized bowl, combine veal, pork, egg, bread crumbs, lemon juice, mint, oregano, salt and pepper. Mix until just combined. Form into 1-inch meatballs and set aside.

2. Heat oil in a large frying pan over medium heat. Add meatballs to the pan without crowding. Fry for 8 to 10 minutes, or until cooked through and golden brown. Reduce heat if necessary. Remove meatballs to a plate and set aside. Repeat with any remaining meatballs, adding more oil if necessary.

Per portion: 64 calories, 6.5 g protein, 3.3 g fat, 0.8 g carbohydrates, 0 g dietary fibre, 9 mg calcium, 0.4 mg iron, 4 mcg folacin

Fresh mint is key to this recipe, but if you can't find it at your store, substitute fresh parsley or basil.

BACON AND CHEDDAR STRATA

MW READER RECIPE: Nothing in the fridge? Try Carolyn Grieve's versatile recipe for a bacon and cheddar strata. No strip of bacon in your fridge? Follow Carolyn's suggestion and substitute back bacon or ham. Out of cheddar cheese? Try Swiss or mozzarella, and substitute zucchini for red pepper, and cooking onions for green onions.

Serves 6

6 slices	egg or french bread (cut into ½-inch thick)
6 slices	bacon
¼	red or green pepper, chopped
2	green onions, sliced
2 cups	grated old cheddar cheese, about 6 oz
3	eggs, lightly beaten
1 ½ cups	milk
1 tsp	Worcestershire sauce
¼ tsp each	salt, black pepper and dry mustard powder

1.   Lightly butter a 9-inch round baking dish. Remove crusts from bread (discard or save to make bread crumbs). Cut bread into ¾-inch cubes. You should have 5 cups. Set aside.

2.   Cook bacon over medium heat in a medium-sized frying pan until crisp, about 10 minutes. Crumble it into ½-inch pieces. Put half the bread cubes in the baking dish. Follow with half the bacon, red pepper, green onion and cheese. Repeat layering, ending with cheese.

3.   In a small bowl, whisk together eggs, milk, Worcestershire sauce, salt, pepper and mustard powder. Pour evenly over bread. Let it stand for at least 30 minutes, but preferably refrigerate a couple of hours or overnight. TIP: If allowed to stand only 30 minutes, the bread will absorb the milk more quickly if you very gently press it into the milk mixture.

4.   Preheat oven to 350F. Bake strata, uncovered, for 40 to 45 minutes or until a knife inserted in the centre comes out clean.

Per portion: 337 calories, 18.4 g protein, 22.5 g fat, 15 g carbohydrates,
0.5 g dietary fibre, 369 mg calcium, 1.4 mg iron

BROILED SALMON WITH
ROASTED RED PEPPER SAUCE

POWER PICK Heart-healthy fish for the family: broiled, baked or poached, fish is an excellent source of lower-fat protein — whether you choose budget-conscious canned tuna or flash-in-the-pan fish fillets.

Serves 2

¼ cup	chicken broth
2	garlic cloves, peeled and coarsely chopped
1 cup	drained, chopped, bottled, roasted red peppers
1 tbsp	balsamic or red wine vinegar
	Pinch of cayenne pepper, or to taste
2 tbsp	chopped fresh basil or parsley
2	salmon steaks (about 6 oz)
1 tsp	olive oil
	Salt and pepper

1. To make Roasted Red Pepper Sauce, simmer chicken broth and garlic in a small saucepan, covered, for 1 minute, until garlic is soft. Add red peppers, vinegar and cayenne pepper. Cover and cook for 2 minutes to blend the flavors. Purée in a blender or food processor. Stir in basil. Reduce heat to low and keep warm while cooking salmon.

2. Preheat broiler. Brush both sides of salmon very lightly with oil and sprinkle with salt and pepper. Place fish on a very lightly oiled rack set over a baking sheet. Broil salmon about 4 inches from the broiler for 3 to 4 minutes. Turn and continue to broil for 3 to 5 minutes, or until salmon is cooked through. Serve with Roasted Red Pepper Sauce drizzled over top.

Per portion: 263 calories, 32.2 g protein, 12.4 g fat, 4.8 g carbohydrates, 0.1 g dietary fibre, 35 mg calcium, 1.8 mg iron, 44 mcg folacin. Excellent source of vitamin B6 and vitamin B12. Good source of vitamin C.

TIPS MW Salmon steaks can also be cooked in a ridged grill pan. Leftover sauce can be served at another meal with vegetables, pasta or chicken.

PORK TENDERLOIN WITH MARMALADE GLAZE

weight SMART Marmalade makes a quick and easy glaze that puts the sizzle in this dish.

Serves 3

¾ lb	pork tenderloin, trimmed of any fat
¼ cup	orange marmalade
2 tsp	Dijon mustard
1 tbsp	red wine vinegar
½ tsp	thyme
	Freshly ground black pepper

1. Preheat oven to 400F. Place pork on a rack set over a foil-lined baking sheet. Stir marmalade with mustard, vinegar and thyme in a small bowl.
2. Spread marmalade mixture over pork. Sprinkle with pepper. Roast for 25 minutes, until the pork reaches 160F on an oven thermometer. The pork should have just a hint of pink when cooked. Slice diagonally into thin slices and serve immediately.

Per serving: 210 calories, 24.2 g protein, 4.2 g fat, 19.2 g carbohydrates, 1.4 g dietary fibre, 24 mg calcium, 1.7 mg iron

TIPS MW If you are interested in nutrition information on topics such as fat, fibre and cholesterol, or if you want ideas on how to eat out nutritiously, contact your local Heart and Stroke office for free pamphlets.

ORIENTAL ORANGE SOLE

weight SMART *MW* READER RECIPE: This reader recipe comes from Christine Cremer of Coquitlam, B.C. Christine is conscious of her fat intake and this is one of her favourite recipes — high in flavor yet low in fat.

Serves 4

1 lb	fresh sole fillets
1 cup	orange juice
2 tbsp	light soy sauce
1 tbsp	minced onion
1 tbsp	brown sugar
2 tsp	ground ginger
2 tsp	cornstarch

1.   In a large frying pan, arrange fish in a single layer, overlapping slightly if necessary. Set aside 2 tablespoons of the orange juice. Stir the remaining orange juice with soy sauce, onion, sugar and ginger in a small bowl. Pour orange juice mixture over fish. Cover and bring to a boil, then reduce heat and simmer gently for 3 to 5 minutes, or until fish flakes with a fork. Remove fish, using a slotted spatula, and place it on a serving plate. Cover loosely to keep warm. Leave the orange juice mixture in the frying pan on stove over medium-high heat.

2.   Stir reserved orange juice with cornstarch in small bowl until cornstarch dissolves. Whisk cornstarch mixture into orange juice mixture, stirring continuously until mixture comes to a boil and sauce thickens. Pour sauce over fish; serve immediately.

> *Per serving: 156 calories, 22.3 g protein, 1.5 g fat, 12.5 g carbohydrates, 0.3 g dietary fibre, 32 mg calcium, 0.8 mg iron*

 Christine says you can also use frozen sole fillets — just thaw and pat dry before using.

BBQ MUSSELS IN BEER

 The first time chef Patrick Bourachot of the Hotel Beauséjour in Moncton, New Brunswick, cooked this recipe, he did it on an open fire at the beach.

Serves 2

2 ½ lb	fresh mussels
3 tbsp	beer or white wine
4	garlic cloves, coarsely chopped
4 sprigs	fresh thyme

1.   Scrub mussels under cold running water to remove beards. Place mussels in the centre of a double-thickness 17 x 20-inch piece of heavy aluminum foil. Sprinkle them with beer and garlic. Put sprigs of thyme on top of mussels. Loosely seal the foil to form a packet (it's important that it be loosely sealed, because the mussels need room to open when they're cooked).

2.   Set the packet on the barbecue over high heat. Cover the barbecue and cook mussels for 8 to 10 minutes. Remove from heat and open packet, discarding any mussels that have not opened. Serve immediately.

> *Per serving: 157 calories, 20.0 g protein, 3.7 g fat, 8.8 g carbohydrates, 0.1 g dietary fibre, 39 mg calcium, 5.6 mg iron. Excellent source of iron.*

BARBECUED TERIYAKI SALMON

Barbecued salmon is a heart-smart alternative to hamburgers.

Serves 4

½ cup	teriyaki sauce
4	chopped green onions
2 tsp	brown sugar
3 large	garlic cloves, sliced
6	thin slices fresh ginger
⅕ lb	salmon fillet, preferably one piece (centre cut)

1.   In a shallow casserole large enough to hold the salmon fillet in a single layer, whisk together teriyaki sauce, green onions, brown sugar, garlic and ginger. Add salmon, turning to coat with mixture. Refrigerate and marinate for 2 hours. Remove salmon from the marinade.

2.   Place the fillet skin side down on a well-greased fish rack, and grill over medium heat. Barbecue for 6 to 10 minutes, depending on the thickness of the fish. Turn fish as little as possible to prevent it from falling apart.

Per portion: 247 calories, 32.1 g protein, 9.9 g fat, 5.8 g carbohydrates,
0.3 g dietary fibre, 33 mg calcium, 1.7 mg iron. Excellent source of
vitamin B6 and vitamin B12. Good source of folacin.

 Cooking times will always vary slightly. Overcooked salmon becomes dry very quickly, so take care not to overcook.

BAKED MUSTARD SALMON

power PICK Salmon, like most fish, is full of nutrients. It is also high in omega-3 fatty acids, which have been linked to lower levels of blood cholesterol.

Serves 2

3 tbsp	Dijon mustard
1 tbsp	finely chopped fresh dill
1 tbsp	lemon juice
	Pinch of salt
	Generous grinding of black pepper
2	salmon steaks, about 1 ½ inches thick

1. Preheat oven to 400F. Stir together Dijon, dill, lemon juice, salt and pepper. Place steaks in a lightly greased shallow casserole dish that's just large enough to hold them.

2. Spread the mustard mixture over both sides of salmon. Bake in a preheated oven for about 15 minutes, or just until salmon flakes with a fork.

> *Per portion: 243 calories, 32.1 g protein, 11.3 g fat, 1.7 g carbohydrates, 49 mg calcium, 1.7 mg iron. Excellent source of vitamin B6 and vitamin B12. Good source of folacin.*

FAMILY-STYLE SKILLET FISH

MW READER RECIPE: "This may not be too exciting," writes Cathy MacIntire. "There are no gourmet ingredients — but it tastes really good and my family asks for it all the time. You can use any white fish you want and it's quick to make," she adds.

Serves 4

19 oz	canned stewed tomatoes
1	garlic clove, minced
1 tsp	fennel seed
½ tsp	thyme
	Pinch of salt and freshly ground black pepper
1	400-g pkg frozen fish fillets, such as haddock
1 cup	thinly sliced zucchini

1. Do not thaw fish. Put tomatoes, garlic and herbs into a large skillet. Bring to a boil over high heat. Reduce heat to a simmer and add the block of frozen fish. Cover and simmer for 10 minutes. Carefully turn fish. Add zucchini and continue to simmer, covered, until fish flakes with a fork, 5 to 6 more minutes.

2. Carefully remove fish to a cutting board (cover with foil to keep warm), leaving the sauce in the pan. Increase the heat to high and boil the sauce for a few minutes to thicken slightly. Cut fish into four pieces and serve with tomato sauce spooned over top.

> *Per portion: 133 calories, 20.6 g protein, 1 g fat, 11.1 g carbohydrates, 2 mg dietary fibre, 96 mg calcium, 2.5 mg iron*

ROAST STUFFED SALMON

 Roasting a whole salmon may seem a little ambitious for a weeknight, but really, it's very easy. The whole recipe will take you only 45 minutes from the refrigerator to the table.

Serves 8

4 lb	whole salmon
	Salt and black pepper
5 sprigs each	fresh parsley and oregano or thyme
2 sprigs	fresh rosemary
1	thinly sliced lemon or lime
2	thinly sliced garlic cloves
2 tbsp	olive oil
1 to 2	cups dry white wine
2	tomatoes, chopped

1.   Preheat oven to 425F. Sprinkle the cavity of salmon with salt and pepper. Lay sprigs of herbs inside cavity, followed by lemon slices and garlic. Close cavity. Place salmon in a roasting pan or on a very large baking sheet just large enough to hold it. Drizzle with olive oil. Sprinkle with salt and pepper, then drizzle with 1 cup wine. Sprinkle tomatoes over fish.

2.   Roast, uncovered, for about 35 minutes (cooking time will vary depending on the size of the fish). If the wine evaporates, add remaining wine. The fish will be cooked when there is no blood coming from the cavity and the flesh flakes with a fork. Once the fish is cooked, place it on a platter. Remove the skin, spoon over any remaining tomato pieces, and serve.

> *Per portion: 264 calories, 31 g protein, 13.3 g fat, 1.9 g carbohydrates, 0.5 mg dietary fibre, 27 mg calcium, 1.6 mg iron. Excellent source of vitamin B6 and vitamin B12. Good source of magnesium and folacin.*

 Use the Canadian cooking method for fish, which is to measure the fish at its thickest point (after stuffing it, if it's a whole fish), then cook for 10 minutes per inch measured.

MUSHROOM GOULASH

MW READER RECIPE: Otto Holzbauer, of Mo-Na Food Enterprises, sells 25 different varieties and blends of wild mushrooms at the Downtown Farmers' Market in Edmonton, Alberta. Otto offered us this recipe for the pick of his crop.

Serves 2 to 3

2 tbsp	butter
1 small	onion, finely chopped
1 lb	mushrooms (preferably oyster), thickly sliced
½ cup	dry white wine
1 tbsp	all-purpose flour
1 cup	vegetable or chicken broth
2 tbsp	sour cream
½ tsp	caraway seeds
½ tsp	salt
2 tbsp	coarsely chopped parsley (optional)
	Freshly ground pepper to taste

1. Melt butter in a large frying pan over medium-high heat. When butter begins to sizzle, add onion and mushrooms; cook for 8 to 10 minutes, stirring frequently, until mushroom juices have evaporated. Add wine and cook, stirring, until evaporated.
2. Sprinkle flour over mushrooms and stir to combine. Add broth and bring to a boil, stirring continuously. Reduce heat and simmer for 1 minute. Remove from heat; stir in the remaining ingredients except parsley until blended. Sprinkle with parsley. Serve with potatoes, egg noodles or rice and a green salad.

Per serving: 153 calories, 3.4 g protein, 9.9 g fat, 10.9 g carbohydrates, 2.8 mg dietary fibre, 33 mg calcium, 2.2 mg iron, 24 mcg folacin. Good source of iron.

This goulash can be prepared in advance. Reheat over a low heat so the sour cream doesn't curdle.

MUSHROOM AND GARLIC PIZZA

Next time you're craving tasty homemade pizza but know you don't have the time or energy to make your own pizza dough — who does these days? — try one of the wonderful frozen pizza doughs, a package mix or a ready-prepared pizza crust.

Serves 4 to 6

2 tbsp	olive or vegetable oil
¾ lb	fresh mushrooms, sliced, including stems
1 tsp	leaf thyme
2	garlic cloves, minced
1 tbsp	coarsely chopped parsley, preferably Italian
¼ tsp	salt
	Freshly ground black pepper to taste
1	28-oz can plum tomatoes, very well drained
2	green onions
¾ cup	coarsely grated mozzarella
2 tbsp	grated Parmesan
1 lb	prepared pizza dough or 12-inch prepared pizza crust

1. Preheat oven to 425F. Oil a 12-inch round pizza pan or a 13 x 9-inch baking sheet. Set aside.
2. Heat oil in a large frying pan over medium heat. Add mushrooms and thyme. Sauté for 5 minutes. Add garlic and continue to sauté for another 3 to 5 minutes or until mushrooms are tender and any juices have evaporated. Remove from heat and stir in parsley, salt and pepper. While mushrooms are cooking, coarsely chop the tomatoes. Drain tomatoes again. They should be very well drained to prevent crust from becoming soggy. Set them aside. Slice green onions and set aside with the grated cheeses.
3. Place the dough directly on the pan. If using a round pan, pat into a 6-inch circle. If using a baking sheet, pat into an 8 x 4-inch rectangle. Using your hands, stretch the dough to the outside edge of the pan and form a slightly thicker rim. Dough can also be rolled out and transferred to the pan. If the dough is difficult to stretch or roll and bounces back, let it rest for about 10 minutes. If using a prepared pizza crust, follow package directions for baking.
4. Scatter the dough with tomatoes. Follow with mushrooms, green onions, mozzarella and Parmesan.
5. Bake 12 to 18 minutes in the centre of the oven until crust is golden brown. After 12 minutes, carefully lift up an edge of the crust to check the underside of the dough. Pizza is ready when dough is golden.

Per servings: 494 calories, 17.2 g protein, 19.3 g fat, 64.3 g carbohydrates, 2.9 mg dietary fibre, 255 mg calcium, 5.0 mg iron.

TIPS If you want to add your very own touch, knead some herbs, chili flakes or a few tablespoons of cheese into the dough. Or to give your crust added texture, sprinkle some cornmeal onto the pan before baking the pizza.

ONE-POT VEGETABLE STEW

power PICK This nutritious meal can be ready in a snap. No-fuss cleanup is a breeze with only one pot to wash.

one POT

Serves 4

1 tbsp	olive oil
1	onion, chopped
2 medium	carrots, cut into ½-inch pieces
1 medium	potato, cut into ½-inch pieces
2	garlic cloves, minced
1 tsp	ground cumin
½ tsp	cinnamon
1	19-oz can Italian-flavored stewed tomatoes
1 small	zucchini, cut into ½-inch chunks
1 small	red pepper, cut into strips
1	19-oz can chickpeas, rinsed and drained
	Salt and pepper to taste

1.   Heat oil in a large saucepan over medium heat. Add onion, carrots, potato, garlic, spices and ¼ cup water. Cook, covered, for 5 minutes, stirring occasionally. Stir in tomatoes, zucchini and red pepper. Cover and simmer for 5 minutes, or until the vegetables are nearly cooked. Uncover, add chickpeas and cook for 5 minutes, until slightly thickened. Add salt and pepper to taste. Serve with rice or couscous, or with crusty bread.

Per portion: 263 calories, 9.9 g protein, 5.5 g fat, 47.2 g carbohydrates, 7.3 mg dietary fibre, 105 mg calcium, 3.1 mg iron. Excellent source of vitamin C. Good source of iron and very high in dietary fibre.

GRILLED CHICKEN, JARLSBERG AND
RED ONION SANDWICH

MW READER RECIPE: "When I was growing up, my favourite sandwich was grilled cheese with lots of ketchup," writes Natalie MacDonald. "It's funny how some things just don't change — I still love grilled cheese, but I've made my new version a bit dressier."

Serves 1

1 ½ tbsp	butter
2 slices	light or dark rye bread
2 tsp	Russian-style or Dijon mustard
1 slice	smoked chicken or turkey (from the deli)
	Jarlsberg or Swiss cheese (from the deli)
2 small	thin slices red onion

1.   Lightly butter one side of one slice of bread. Spread the other side with mustard. Top with chicken or turkey, folding the slice to fit the size of bread if necessary. Thinly slice about three pieces of cheese to fit on the bread in a single layer. Top with red onion slices. Spread one side of the remaining slice of bread with mustard. Lay bread mustard side down on top of onion slices to form a sandwich. Lightly butter the outside of the top bread slice.
2.   Place the sandwich in a small frying pan over medium-low heat. Cook for 3 to 5 minutes per side, or until golden brown on both sides.

Per portion: 403 calories, 20.5 g protein, 23 g fat, 31.1 g carbohydrates, 2 mg dietary fibre, 349 mg calcium, 1.5 mg iron

SMOKED TURKEY WRAP

There's no need to panic when you just can't get a hot dinner on the table. These delicious wraps, served with soup or salad, make a healthy and filling meal.

Serves 4

8 to 12	medium asparagus
4 small	leaves lettuce
4	8-inch flour tortillas
4	thin slices cooked smoked turkey or chicken
½ cup	thin strips of bottled red peppers, patted dry
⅓ cup each	coarsely grated carrot and zucchini
2 tbsp	coarsely chopped basil leaves
⅓ cup	crumbled goat's or feta cheese

1. Lay asparagus flat in a wide frying pan in a shallow amount of water. Cook until barely tender — about 2 minutes. Drain and rinse under cold water; pat dry.

2. Place one lettuce leaf over each tortilla, then cover with one slice of smoked turkey. Lay ¼ each of the red pepper strips, carrots, zucchini and basil, two or three asparagus spears and ¼ of the cheese in the centre of the tortillas. Fold the bottom of tortilla over the filling and then roll up. Repeat with remaining tortillas and filling. Secure with a toothpick. Serve within one hour, or wrap in plastic and refrigerate overnight.

Per wrap: 224 calories, 12.2 g protein, 6.9 g fat, 29.2 g carbohydrates, 2.2 mg dietary fibre, 135 mg calcium, 2.6 mg iron, 59 mcg folacin. Excellent source of vitamin A, vitamin C and folacin. Good source of iron. Moderate in dietary fibre.

HOT MEATBALLS ON A CRUSTY ITALIAN BUN

There's nothing like a messy meatball sandwich to brighten up your family's mid-week meal.

Serves 4

½ lb	lean ground beef
½ lb	ground pork
1	egg, lightly beaten
3 tbsp	finely chopped onion
1 tbsp	finely chopped parsley
1 tsp each	basil and salt
½ tsp	oregano
	Generous grinding of black pepper
1 tbsp	olive or vegetable oil
1 cup	homemade or store-bought meatless spaghetti sauce with mushrooms
4 slices	mozzarella (optional)
	Hot banana peppers (optional)
4	crusty Italian buns, split in half

1. In a medium-sized bowl, combine meat, egg, onion, parsley, basil, salt, oregano and pepper. Form meat into 1 ½-inch balls, then set aside on a piece of waxed paper.
2. Heat oil in a large wide saucepan over medium heat. When oil is hot, add meatballs in a single layer. Brown on all sides, turning gently, for 5 to 6 minutes. Do not overcrowd pan; if necessary, cook in two batches. Remove meatballs from the pan and drain all the fat from the pan.
3. Return meatballs to the pan and add spaghetti sauce. Gently stir meatballs so they are evenly covered in sauce. Bring the mixture to a boil, cover, then reduce heat to low. Simmer for about 10 minutes, stirring occasionally, until meatballs are cooked through. This can be prepared a day in advance. Refrigerate, then reheat, covered, over medium-low heat.
4. Place a slice of mozzarella, if using, on the bottom half of each bun. Then spoon about 5 meatballs and some sauce over cheese. Top with hot peppers if using. Place the tops of the buns to form sandwiches. Serve immediately.

Per portion: 490 calories, 30 g protein, 19 g fat, 48.2 g carbohydrates, 1.4 mg dietary fibre, 71 mg calcium, 3.8 mg iron

WILD RICE AND CHICKEN CASSEROLE

MW READER RECIPE: This recipe comes from Elaine Kolenosky of Calgary, Alberta. It's a great meal to serve a hungry crowd.

Serves 6

1	180-g pkg long grain and wild rice mix
1 tbsp	vegetable or olive oil
3	boneless, skinless chicken breasts, cut into bite-sized pieces
2 cups each	small cauliflower and broccoli florets
1 cup	thinly sliced mushrooms
1	10-oz can undiluted mushroom soup
⅓ cup	milk
2 tbsp	white wine or sherry
2 cups	grated cheddar cheese
	Black pepper to taste

1. Prepare rice according to package directions. Meanwhile, heat oil in a large frying pan over medium-high heat. Add chicken and cook for about 5 minutes until golden and cooked through. Set aside. Bring a large pot of salted water to a boil. Add cauliflower and cook for 1 minute. Add broccoli to the water and cook for 2 minutes. Drain the vegetables and rinse under cold running water to stop the cooking; drain well.
2. Preheat oven to 350F. In a casserole dish, combine cooked rice, chicken, vegetables, mushrooms, mushroom soup, milk, wine, cheese and pepper. Bake, covered, in a preheated oven for 15 minutes. Remove cover and continue to bake for 10 to 15 minutes, until hot.

Per portion: 520 calories, 23.6 g protein, 25.2 g fat, 49.5 g carbohydrates,
5.2 g dietary fibre, 64 mg calcium, 4 mg iron

FISH IN BATTER

MW READER RECIPE: Eleanor Green, from Grand Manan, New Brunswick, works on the social committee for her United Baptist church, organizing church suppers for family and friends. The suppers — often for more than 150 people — are held both for fun and fundraising, and dishes are assigned to all families. The only requirement: they must all be easy to reheat and serve. Here is one of Eleanor's farvourite recipes.

Serves 4

1 ¼ lb	pollock, haddock or cod fillets, preferably fresh
	Vegetable oil for frying
¾ cup	all-purpose flour
1 ¼ tsp	baking powder
2 tsp	dried chives
½ tsp	salt
	Pinch of baking soda
	Pinch of granulated sugar
½ to ⅔	cup water
1 tsp	white vinegar

1. If fish is frozen, thaw before use. Pat dry to remove as much excess moisture as possible. Pour about 4 inches of oil into a large deep saucepan or deep fryer. Heat until it reaches about 375F on a thermometer, or until a piece of bread dropped in turns golden brown after 20 seconds.
2. In a large shallow dish, stir together flour, baking powder, chives, salt, baking soda and sugar until mixed. Whisk ½ cup water with vinegar until blended, then whisk it into the dry ingredients. The batter should be like a thick pancake batter. If the batter is too thick, add a bit more water.
3. Coat both sides of fish with batter (it does not need to cover fish perfectly). Add fish to oil one or two fillets at a time. Do not crowd the pan. Fish will take 3 to 5 minutes to cook, depending on thickness. Remove it from pan and place on paper towels to absorb any excess oil. It is best served immediately with a green salad. To reheat, place in a single layer on a baking sheet (do not crowd). Heat uncovered at 300F.

Per portion: 280 calories, 29.3 g protein, 9.1 g fat , 18.5 g carbohydrates, 0.7 mg dietary fibre, 90 mg calcium, 2.5 mg iron. Excellent source of vitamin B12 and iron.

 You can double this recipe for a hungry crowd.

MAGIC WITH LEFTOVERS

Making food appetizing the second day is a real challenge. No one wants to waste food, but picky eaters are sure to turn their noses up at a dinner that looks too much like something they've seen the day before. It takes imagination to turn yesterday's turkey into today's Turkey Manicotti or Sunday's roast into Shepherd's Pie.

This chapter contains 11 recipes to help you transform leftovers into fresh new meals everyone can enjoy. Now you can feel free to make a big old-fashioned family dinner on the weekend because you'll be able to use these recipes to turn what's left into quick and easy mid-week meals.

SCALLOPED POTATOES WITH LEFTOVER HAM

The baked ham you served for Sunday dinner can be disguised on Monday in a brand-new treat.

Serves 8

1 large	onion, finely chopped
1 cup	finely chopped leftover cooked ham (about 4 oz)
2 ½ cups	lightly packed grated Gruyère or Swiss cheese (about 8 oz)
3 tbsp	all-purpose flour
2 lb	medium potatoes (about 6 or 7), peeled and very thinly sliced
	Salt and black pepper
1 cup each	milk and whipping cream

1. Preheat oven to 350F. Lightly grease a 9-inch square shallow casserole. Toss onion and ham together in a small bowl. In a separate bowl, toss cheese with flour.

2. Layer a quarter of potato slices on the bottom of the casserole. Sprinkle with salt, pepper and a quarter of the ham mixture. Then sprinkle with one-quarter of the cheese mixture. Repeat, layering three more times, ending with cheese. Heat milk with cream in a small saucepan until hot. Pour it over potatoes. Cover the casserole and bake for 30 minutes, until potatoes are nearly tender. Uncover and continue to bake for 25 to 30 minutes until potatoes are tender and cheese is golden brown.

Per portion: 358 calories, 16.7 g protein, 22 g fat, 24 g carbohydrates, 1.5 mg dietary fibre, 4.9 mg calcium, 0.7 mg iron. Excellent source of calcium.

LEFTOVER BEEF SHEPHERD'S PIE

Here's a great idea for combining the remains of a roast beef dinner with extra ground beef or ground lamb.

Serves 4

5	baking potatoes, peeled and quartered
¼ cup	milk
2 tbsp	butter
	Generous pinch of nutmeg
	Salt and pepper to taste
2 tbsp	olive oil
2 medium	onions, chopped
1 medium	carrot, finely chopped
1 medium	celery stalk, finely chopped
1 tsp	dried thyme
¼ tsp	chili flakes
1 lb	extra-lean ground beef or ground lamb
2 cups	diced cooked roast beef (¼-inch cubes)
3 tbsp	all-purpose flour
⅓ cup	beef broth
2 tbsp	tomato paste
2 tsp	Worcestershire sauce

1. Put potatoes in a large saucepan of cold salted water. Bring to a boil and cook, partially covered, for 20 minutes. Drain. Mash potatoes with milk, butter, nutmeg, salt and pepper until well mixed.
2. Preheat oven to 375F. Heat oil in a large frying pan over medium heat. Add onions, carrot, celery, thyme and chili flakes. Cook for 5 minutes. Add ground beef; cook, stirring frequently until no longer pink. Stir in roast beef. Stir in flour, then beef broth, tomato paste, Worcestershire sauce, salt and pepper to taste. Reduce heat and cook, uncovered, for 5 minutes.
3. Spread the meat mixture in a 9-inch square casserole. Top with mashed potatoes. Bake for 35 to 45 minutes. Place under the broiler for 1 minute to brown potatoes slightly.

Per serving: 348 calories, 25.1 g protein, 15.5 g fat, 26.8 g carbohydrates, 2.4 mg dietary fibre, 39 mg calcium, 3 mg iron. Good source of iron.

If you have gravy left over from the roast beef, use it instead of the beef broth for even better flavor.

LEFTOVER TURKEY MANICOTTI

Leftover turkey gets a whole new spin when added to this terrific pasta recipe.

Serves 6 to 8

1	225-g pkg manicotti (about 14)
1 tsp	vegetable oil
1	700 mL jar meatless spaghetti sauce
⅓ cup	salsa
1 cup	grated mozzarella cheese
1 cup	grated old cheddar cheese
1	300-g pkg chopped frozen spinach, thawed
1 cup	ricotta cheese
1	egg, lightly beaten
¼ cup	finely chopped coriander
2 tsp	finely chopped jalapeño pepper (about 1)
4 cups	finely chopped cooked turkey

1. Cook manicotti according to package directions. Be careful not to overcook or they will fall apart during baking. Once cooked, rinse immediately under cold running water. Drain well, toss with oil and set aside.

2. Preheat oven to 375F. Stir spaghetti sauce with salsa; set aside. Stir mozzarella with cheddar in a large bowl; set aside. Squeeze spinach to remove all water, then stir it with ricotta, egg, coriander, jalapeño and half of the cheese mixture. Stir in turkey until well blended.

3. Stuff manicotti with the turkey mixture. Spoon about 1 cup of the spaghetti sauce mixture onto the bottom of a 13 x 9-inch casserole dish. Place the stuffed manicotti in a single layer on the sauce. Spread the remaining spaghetti sauce mixture over manicotti, then sprinkle with the remaining cheese. Bake uncovered for 35 to 45 minutes.

Per manicotti: 289 calories, 21.6 g protein, 12.5 g fat, 22.4 g carbohydrates, 2.3 mg dietary fibre, 194 mg calcium, 1.7 mg iron. Good source of magnesium and calcium. Moderate in dietary fibre.

STIR-FRIED RICE WITH LEFTOVER PORK

 This recipe works best if you use rice that is left over from the day before.

Serves 8

2 tbsp	vegetable oil
1 small	onion, cut into ¼-inch pieces
1 medium	carrot, cut into ¼-inch pieces
1 small	celery stalk, cut into ¼-inch pieces
4 cups	cold cooked white or brown rice
1 ½ cups	diced cooked pork (½-inch cubes)
2	eggs, lightly beaten
2 tbsp	oyster sauce
1 ½ tbsp	soy sauce
¼ cup	fresh or frozen peas
1	green onion, thinly sliced

1. Heat oil in a large frying pan or wok over medium-high heat. Add onion, carrot and celery, and cook for about 2 minutes, stirring continuously, just until barely tender.

2. Meanwhile, use a fork to fluff the rice into separate grains. Add rice to the frying pan and cook, stirring frequently, for 3 to 5 minutes until nearly heated through. Add pork and continue to cook for 1 minute, until pork is hot. Make a well in the centre of the rice mixture. Pour eggs, oyster sauce and soy sauce into the well, and stir continuously until eggs are softly scrambled. Stir in peas and green onion and cook until just heated through.

Per serving: 217 calories, 12.4 g protein, 7.1 g fat, 24.9 g carbohydrates, 1.1 mg dietary fibre, 35 mg calcium, 1 mg iron

 Oyster sauce can be purchased in the Oriental section of most grocery stores and Chinese supermarkets. If using frozen peas, it is not necessary to thaw them before adding them to the rice.

HOMEMADE SOUP

Next time — and every time — you have leftover vegetables, meat or pasta, pack it in a freezer bag to save for making soup. It will taste better than anything you can buy, and you'll be able to control the salt and fat content as well.

Makes about 18 cups

1 tbsp	olive oil
1	onion, chopped
2	garlic cloves, minced
1	carrot, finely diced
1 stalk	celery, finely diced
10 to 12 cups	chicken, vegetable or beef broth, vegetable cooking water, or a combination
1 cup	uncooked small pasta shapes such as stars or elbows or bite-sized pieces of spaghetti or egg noodles
1 ½ cups	diced uncooked vegetables such as potato, zucchini or carrots
1 ½ cups	cooked dried beans or 1 19-oz can beans, rinsed
1 ½ cups	combination diced cooked leftover vegetables such as beans, squash, cauliflower and spinach, or frozen corn or peas
⅓ cup	chopped parsley (optional)
	Salt and pepper to taste

1.   Heat oil in a very large saucepan over medium heat. Add onion, garlic, carrot and celery; cook until tender. Add 10 cups of broth and bring to a boil. Add pasta and uncooked vegetables. Cook, partially covered, stirring frequently until pasta and vegetables are tender.

2.   Add cooked or canned beans, cooked leftover vegetables and parsley. Reduce heat and cook, covered, for about 30 minutes to blend flavors. Add salt and pepper to taste. If necessary, thin with remaining broth. Recipe can be halved.

Per portion: 114 calories, 6.5 g protein, 2.1 g fat, 17.5 g carbohydrates, 2.6 mg dietary fibre, 30 mg calcium, 1.1 mg iron, 36 mcg folacin. Good source of vitamin A and folacin. Moderate in dietary fibre.

Leftover cooked vegetables make great thick soups. Sauté chopped onion and garlic in a tablespoon of olive oil in a large saucepan until tender. Add leftover cooked vegetables — potato, cauliflower, squash, carrots, or any combination — and a couple of cups of chicken broth. Cover and cook until vegetables are very tender. Purée until smooth. For added flavor, cook the vegetables for the soup in bacon drippings. Or add bits of leftover chicken, pork, smoked ham or salami to the soup. You can also add the rind from a chunk of Parmesan to the soup while it cooks or sprinkle grated Parmesan over just before serving.

QUICK LEFTOVER TURKEY POT PIE

Mashed potatoes create a quick and easy crust for this great leftover meal.

Serves 8

¼ cup	butter
1	onion, chopped
2 tsp	rosemary leaves, crumbled
¼ cup	all-purpose flour
1 ½ cup	chicken broth
½ cup	milk
1 tbsp	Dijon mustard
2 cups	large frozen mixed vegetables, such as California Blend
2 cups	bite-sized pieces of cooked turkey
¼ cup	chopped parsley
3 to 4 cups	leftover mashed potatoes

1. Preheat oven to 375F. Melt butter in a large saucepan over medium heat. Add onion and rosemary and cook, stirring frequently, until onion is soft. Stir in flour until combined. Gradually whisk in chicken broth, milk and Dijon, making sure there are no lumps. Bring the mixture to a boil, reduce heat to low and cook, stirring frequently, for a couple of minutes.
2. Stir in frozen vegetables, turkey and parsley. Heat until mixture is hot. Turn into a 9- or 10-inch pie plate. Thinly spread potatoes over the top of the mixture. Place the pie plate on a baking tray to catch any drips. Bake, uncovered, for 30 to 40 minutes, or until the turkey mixture and mashed potatoes are hot.

Per portion: 250 calories, 15.3 g protein, 11.1 g fat, 22.7 g carbohydrates, 3.3 mg dietary fibre, 84 mg calcium, 1.5 mg iron, 18 mcg folacin. Excellent source of vitamin A. Good source of zinc. Moderate in dietary fibre.

CLASSIC TURKEY POT PIE

A leftover as traditional as your Thanksgiving dinner!

Serves 8

¼ cup	butter
1	onion, chopped
2	garlic cloves, minced
⅓ cup	all-purpose flour
1 ½ cups	chicken broth
½ cup	whipping cream
¼ cup	dry white wine
1 tbsp	dried tarragon
2 cups	bite-sized pieces of cooked turkey
2 small	potatoes (preferably red-skinned), unpeeled, cooked and cut into ½-inch pieces
2	carrots, cooked and thinly sliced
½ cup	frozen peas
	Salt and pepper to taste
1	9-inch frozen deep-dish pie shell, thawed

1.   Preheat oven to 400F. Melt butter over medium heat. Add onion and garlic; cook just until onion is soft. Stir in flour until combined. Whisk in broth, cream, wine and tarragon, making sure there are no flour lumps. Bring the mixture to a boil, reduce heat to low and cook for a couple of minutes, stirring frequently. The mixture will be very thick.
2.   Stir in turkey, potatoes, carrots, peas, salt and pepper. Heat through. Turn into a 9-inch pie plate. Carefully remove the pastry from the aluminum pie plate. Place it on top of the turkey filling, trying not to tear it. If the pastry tears a bit, gently pinch it back together. Using the tip of a knife, cut three slits in the centre of the pastry. Place the pie plate on a baking tray to catch any drips. Bake, uncovered, for about 25 minutes, or until the filling is hot and pastry is golden brown.

Per portion: 370 calories, 15.2 g protein, 22.4 g fat, 26.6 g carbohydrates, 2 mg dietary fibre, 43 mg calcium, 2.1 mg iron, 20 mcg folacin. Excellent source of vitamin A. Good source of vitamin B6, iron and zinc. Moderate in dietary fibre.

Barbecued
Teriyaki Salmon

Page 98

One-Pot
Vegetable Stew

Page 103

Homemade Soup

Page 114

**Family-Style
Meal-in-One**

Page 120

David Chilton's
(aka The Wealthy Barber)
Burger Alarm

Page 121

Individual
Ice Cream
Truffle Bombes

Page 146

Quick Strawberry
Sauce for Cake

Page 146

Quick Coffee Pie

Page 145

Very Berry Cherry Cobbler

Page 150

Chocolate
Pecan Pie

Page 152

Amazing
Oatmeal Cookies

Page 168

Pineapple
Squares

Page 170

Bonanzas

Page 171

**Aunt Lila's
Drop Cookies**

Page 172

MEDITERRANEAN TURKEY PIE

Fresh vegetables make this a healthy choice.

Serves 8

1 tbsp	olive oil
1	red pepper, cored and cut into thin julienne strips
1	green pepper, cored and cut into thin julienne strips
1 small	zucchini, sliced (about 1 ½ cups)
2 cups	unpeeled ½-inch cubes of eggplant
1 cup	sliced mushrooms
2	garlic cloves, minced
1 tbsp	Italian seasoning
½ tsp	salt
1	19-oz can tomatoes, drained and crushed
2 cups	bite-sized pieces of cooked turkey
⅓ cup	finely grated Romano or Parmesan cheese
2 tbsp	chopped pitted black olives
1	9-inch frozen deep-dish pie shell, thawed

1.   Preheat oven to 400F. Heat oil in a large frying pan over medium heat. Add red and green peppers, zucchini, eggplant, mushrooms, garlic and seasonings; cook, stirring frequently, until vegetables are very tender — about 20 minutes. Stir in tomatoes, turkey, cheese and olives.

2.   Turn into a 9-inch pie plate. Carefully remove the pastry from the aluminum pie plate. Place it on top of the turkey filling, trying not to tear it. If the pastry tears a bit, gently pinch it back together. Place the pie plate on a baking tray to catch any drips. Bake, uncovered, in the centre of the oven for about 25 minutes, or until the filling is hot and pastry is golden brown.

Per portion: 262 calories, 14.5 g protein, 14.4 g fat, 19.2 g carbohydrates, 2.4 mg dietary fibre, 84 mg calcium, 2.1 mg iron, 20 mcg folacin. Excellent source of vitamin C. Good source of vitamin B6, iron and zinc. Moderate in dietary fibre.

For a change of pace, roll out thawed frozen puff pastry to cover the pie filling and bake according to package directions.

EXOTICALLY SPICED TURKEY POT PIE

A real change from traditional pot pie, this recipe will add variety and spice to your weekly meal plan.

Serves 8

Filling

1 tbsp	butter
1	onion, finely chopped
2	garlic cloves, minced
1 tsp	minced peeled ginger
1 tsp	whole cumin seeds
¼ tsp	ground coriander
5	whole cloves
1	19-oz can tomatoes (including juice), crushed
1 cup	uncooked frozen or cooked fresh cauliflower florets
½ cup	frozen peas
¼ tsp	cayenne
2 cups	bite-sized pieces of cooked turkey

Crust

3 cups	cooked rice
2	eggs, lightly beaten
¼ cup each	yogurt and finely chopped coriander

1. Preheat oven to 375F. Melt butter in a large frying pan over medium heat. Add onion, garlic, ginger and spices; cook, stirring frequently, until onion is soft. Add tomatoes, cauliflower, peas and cayenne; cook, covered, for 5 minutes to allow flavors to blend. Stir in turkey.

2. Turn into a 9-inch pie plate. Stir together rice, eggs, yogurt and coriander. Spoon the rice mixture over the turkey filling, spreading evenly. Place the pie plate on a baking tray to catch any drips. Bake, uncovered, for 30 to 35 minutes until the filling and rice are hot.

Per portion: 227 calories, 15.9 g protein, 5.2 g fat, 28.7 g carbohydrates, 1.9 mg dietary fibre, 67 mg calcium, 1.8 mg iron, 28 mcg folacin. Good source of vitamin B6 and zinc.

MACARONI AND CHEESE

PICK Have you got a fridge full of leftover bits of cheese and a cupboard full of not-quite-empty boxes of pasta? Here's how to put them together for a quick and easy dinner.

Serves 6

5 to 6 cups	dried penne, fusilli or rotini (or a combination of noodles)
3 tbsp	butter
3 tbsp	all-purpose flour
1 tsp	dry mustard powder
	Generous pinch of nutmeg and cayenne
2 ¼ cups	milk
	Salt and pepper to taste
3 cups	grated leftover cheese, such as cheddar, mozzarella, Parmesan, Gouda or Swiss

1. Bring a large pot of salted water to a boil. Cook pasta for about 8 minutes, or until tender. Drain well. Turn into a medium-sized casserole dish. Preheat oven to 350F.
2. Meanwhile, melt butter in a medium-sized saucepan over medium heat. Stir in the flour, mustard powder, nutmeg and cayenne. Cook for about 30 seconds, or until flour begins to bubble. Gradually whisk in milk. Stirring continuously, bring the liquid to a boil. Reduce heat to low and simmer for 1 minute. Season with salt and pepper.
3. Reserve ½ cup of cheese, and gradually add the rest, about ½ cup at a time, stirring until completely melted. Toss the sauce with the pasta; sprinkle with the reserved cheese. Bake until the cheese is melted, about 15 minutes, or cover and refrigerate to bake later.

Per serving: 628 calories, 28.9 g protein, 25.1 g fat, 70.4 g carbohydrates, 3.6 mg dietary fibre, 579 mg calcium, 1.6 mg iron. Excellent source of vitamin A, vitamin B12, calcium and zinc. Moderate amount of dietary fibre.

Adding a couple of tablespoons of salsa, chopped green onions or leftover chicken gives your macaroni and cheese a whole new flavor. If you are using a combination of pastas, choose varieties that cook in more or less the same amount of time. As for the combination of cheeses, the macaroni will taste best if one of the cheeses has a strong flavor, such as old cheddar or Parmesan.

FAMILY-STYLE MEAL-IN-ONE

PICK *power* **POT** *one* If you use leftover cooked broccoli, add it during the last few minutes of cooking. If you use fresh broccoli florets, add them halfway through the cooking.

Serves 4

1 tbsp	vegetable or olive oil
2 cups	sliced mushrooms (about 4 oz)
1	onion, chopped
1 lb	extra-lean ground chicken
1 cup	uncooked long-grain rice
2 cups	chicken broth
2 cups	frozen broccoli florets, cut into bite-sized pieces
1 cup	coarsely grated cheddar cheese (optional)

1. Heat oil in a large saucepan over medium heat. Add mushrooms and onion; cook until mushrooms soften. Add chicken and cook, stirring frequently, until it is cooked through.

2. Add rice, stirring until mixed in with chicken. Add broth, bring the mixture to a boil, then cover and simmer gently for 20 to 25 minutes until the liquid is absorbed. Stir broccoli into the rice mixture during the last 7 minutes of cooking. Stir in cheese just before serving.

Per portion: 453 calories, 30.7 g protein, 16.2 g fat (32% calories from fat), 45.1 g carbohydrates, 3.7 g dietary fibre, 74 mg calcium, 2.6 mg iron, 48 mcg folacin. Excellent source of vitamin C, vitamin B6 and zinc. Good source of vitamin A and folacin. Moderate dietary fibre.

CELEBRITY BURGERS

The Great Canadian Burger is a favourite food with everyone from Boy Scouts to big-name stars. Ever wonder how Canada's famous players like to eat their burgers? We did — and we turned our curiosity into an annual feature about just that. Over the last few years, we've asked dozens of celebrities about their hamburger preferences and here's a taste of the answers we received.

Elvis Stojko told us all about his mom's hamburger recipe and Céline Dion gave us the inside scoop on the burgers served at her restaurant chain. David Chilton, The Wealthy Barber, provided us with a Looney low-fat Burger Alarm and Bryan Adams gave us the skinny on his favourite all-veggie burger. Check out the next chapter for the best of five years of Famous Canadians' Favourite Burgers.

ATOM EGOYAN'S SPICED BURGER

Award-winning movie director Atom Egoyan is probably best known for his films *Exotica* and *The Sweet Hereafter*. Cairo-born, of Armenian descent, Atom was raised in B.C. With as varied a background as his, it's no wonder Atom's burger is unique.

Makes 4 burgers

1 tbsp	olive oil
1	onion, finely chopped
2 large	garlic cloves, minced
1 tbsp	ground cumin
2 small	tomatoes, peeled, seeded and chopped
	Salt and freshly ground black pepper to taste
1 lb	lean ground beef
1	egg, lightly beaten
3 tbsp to ⅓ cup	dried bread crumbs
4	toasted pita or kaiser buns

1. Heat oil in a medium-sized frying pan over medium heat. Add onion, garlic, cumin and tomatoes and cook, stirring occasionally, until tomatoes become soft and paste-like and the juice has evaporated. Cool completely. Season with salt and pepper.
2. Blend the tomato mixture with ground beef, egg and 3 tablespoons of bread crumbs. If the mixture is too moist and doesn't hold together, add more bread crumbs. Form into four patties. Place them on a greased, preheated grill and barbecue for 5 to 7 minutes per side until cooked through. Serve inside a pita or kaiser bun.

Per portion: 459 calories, 30.4 g protein, 18.2 g fat, 42 g carbohydrates, 1.5 mg dietary fibre, 92 mg calcium, 5.6 mg iron. An excellent source of iron.

In a pinch, Atom suggests substituting a couple of tablespoons of tomato paste for the tomatoes and eliminating the bread crumbs.

TED ROGERS'S ISLAND BURGERS

Ted Rogers may be a multimedia visionary, but when it comes to relaxing, he and his wife, Loretta, spend as much time as they can at their island cottage in Muskoka. Loretta is a creative cook who loves to experiment, and she came up with this delicious recipe that features summer's fresh herbs.

Makes 4 burgers

1 lb	ground beef, ground veal or ground chicken
1	egg, lightly beaten

Stuffing

2 slices	sandwich bread
½ small	onion, finely chopped
½ tsp	poultry seasoning
1	garlic clove, minced
	Salt and pepper to taste
2 tbsp	chopped fresh basil
2 tbsp	chopped fresh parsley
	Grated cheddar cheese to top burgers
4	toasted kaiser or sesame-seed buns

1. Mix beef with egg until blended. Divide into four balls and set aside.
2. Make the stuffing by pulsing bread in a food processor until finely ground. Add onion, poultry seasoning, garlic, salt, pepper, basil and parsley and blend until well combined.
3. Make a well in the centre of each meatball. Fill the cavity with the stuffing, then pinch the meat until the filling is sealed in. Flatten each meatball into a burger shape.
4. Barbecue on a greased, preheated grill for 5 to 7 minutes per side until cooked through. Top with cheese and serve in buns.

Per portion: 477 calories, 27.5 g protein, 19.5 g fat, 45.7 g carbohydrates, 1.6 mg dietary fibre, 62 mg calcium, 4.1 mg iron. An excellent source of iron.

GRAHAM GREENE'S BURGER

Actor Graham Greene is known for his roles in countless movie and theatre productions. Graham makes his burgers as follows: "Smash it, crush it, mix it, make patties, cook them, eat them and serve with a light red wine."

Makes 6 burgers

1 lb	lean ground beef
½ lb	lean ground pork
1 small	onion, finely chopped
½ small	green pepper, finely chopped
1 small stalk	celery, finely chopped
2 tbsp	tomato paste
2 tsp	Worcestershire sauce
3 large	garlic cloves, minced
	Salt and pepper to taste
6	toasted sesame-seed buns

1. Mix all the ingredients (except buns) together until combined. Form into six patties.
2. Barbecue on a greased preheated grill for 5 to 7 minutes per side until cooked through. Serve in sesame-seed buns.

Per serving: 379 calories, 26 g protein, 14.3 g fat, 35.1 g carbohydrates, 1.8 mg dietary fibre, 60 mg calcium, 3.4 mg iron. An excellent source of iron.

MARILYN BROOKS'S TERIYAKI BURGER

Marilyn Brooks is a giant in the Canadian fashion industry. The inspiration for her burger was a trip to Hawaii — she's been hooked ever since.

Makes 4 burgers

1 lb	lean ground beef
½ pkg	onion soup mix (about 2 tbsp)
1	egg, lightly beaten
	Salt and freshly ground black pepper
4	toasted sesame-seed buns
	Toppings: mayonnaise, lettuce, tomato and pineapple slices, teriyaki sauce

1.   Combine beef, onion soup mix, egg, salt and pepper until blended. Form into four patties.
2.   Place on a greased preheated grill and barbecue for 5 to 7 minutes per side until cooked through. Meanwhile, spread each bun with mayonnaise and top with lettuce, tomato and a slice of pineapple. Place a burger on each bun and sprinkle generously with teriyaki sauce.

> *Per serving: 387 calories, 27.2 g protein, 14.6 g fat, 34.8 g carbohydrates, 1.4 mg dietary fibre, 64 mg calcium, 3.7 mg iron. An excellent source of iron.*

MR. DRESSUP'S BURGER

Mr. Dressup (aka Ernie Coombs) has been watched by millions of children around the world for 30 years. When it comes to making burgers, he's nutritionally conscious: he tries to restrict fat in his diet, so his recipe uses lean beef and turkey.

Makes 8 burgers

1 lb	extra-lean ground beef
1 lb	ground turkey or chicken
½	red onion, finely chopped (about ⅓ cup)
¼	medium green pepper, finely chopped (about ¼ cup)
1 cup	finely chopped mushrooms (about 7 mushrooms)
3	garlic cloves, finely minced
2 slices	crumbled whole wheat bread
1 tsp	freshly ground black pepper
	Worcestershire sauce or Picapeppa sauce
8	toasted hamburger buns
	Garnish: lettuce, tomato and light mayonnaise

1.   Using your hands or a spoon, mix all the ingredients (except Worcestershire sauce and buns) together until well combined. Form into eight patties.
2.   Barbecue the burgers for 5 to 7 minutes a side, sprinkling them with Worcestershire sauce as you're grilling them (make sure burgers are well cooked as they contain poultry meat). Serve on toasted hamburger buns with lettuce, tomato and mayonnaise.

> *Per serving: 390 calories, 26.1 g protein, 14.1 g fat, 38.6 g carbohydrates, 2.2 mg dietary fibre, 70 mg calcium, 3.7 mg iron. Excellent source of iron. Moderate in dietary fibre.*

CÉLINE DION'S BURGER BY NICKELS

Céline Dion may be an international sensation but she remains firmly rooted in Canada. In fact, her burger recipe comes from Nickels, one of ten '50s-style restaurants in Montreal that she owns with three other partners.

Makes 4 burgers

1 lb	ground beef
1 tbsp	dried basil
1 tsp each	paprika, dried oregano and dried rosemary
½ tsp each	salt and black pepper
4	toasted sesame-seed buns
	Toppings: tomatoes, Canadian back bacon, onions and mustard

1. Using your hands or a spoon, mix all the ingredients (except buns) until well combined.
2. Barbecue for 5 to 7 minutes per side, or until cooked through. Serve in sesame-seed buns with toppings.

Per serving: 379 calories, 26 g protein, 14.3 g fat, 35.1 g carbohydrates, 1.8 mg dietary fibre, 60 mg calcium, 3.4 mg iron. An excellent source of iron.

MANON RHEAUME'S BURGER

Manon Rheaume became an instant celebrity as the first female ever to play in the NHL. Manon eats food with low fat content and says she has "never felt better," feeling strong in mind and body.

Makes 4 burgers

1 lb	ground turkey or chicken
1	egg, lightly beaten
3 tbsp	dried bread crumbs
1 tbsp	Dijon mustard
1 tsp	Worcestershire sauce
¼ tsp	Tabasco
½ tsp each	salt and pepper
4	whole wheat hamburger buns

1.   Using your hands or a spoon, mix all the ingredients (except hamburger buns) together in a large bowl until well combined. Form into four patties.
2.   Barbecue the burgers for 5 to 7 minutes per side, making sure the burgers are well cooked as they contain poultry meat. Serve with your favourite toppings on whole wheat buns.

Per portion: 383 calories, 28.4 g protein, 14.6 g fat, 35.7 g carbohydrates, 3.6 mg dietary fibre, 99 mg calcium, 3.4 mg iron. Good source of iron. Moderate in dietary fibre.

PETER MANSBRIDGE'S WEEKEND BURGER

CBC's anchor Peter Mansbridge heads to his year-round cabin when it's time to relax. Barbecuing is a big deal, especially during the summer when everything from fish to chicken to burgers gets thrown on the grill. Fresh herbs are what make this burger especially good.

Makes 8 burgers

2 lb	ground beef
1	egg, lightly beaten
1 medium	onion, finely chopped
2	garlic cloves, minced
2 tbsp each	finely chopped parsley and oregano
1 tbsp	finely chopped fresh sage
¾ tsp each	salt and black pepper
8	toasted sesame-seed buns

1.   Using your hands or a spoon, mix all the ingredients (except hamburger buns) together in a large bowl until well combined. Form into eight patties.
2.   Barbecue the burgers for 5 to 7 minutes per side, or until cooked through. Serve with your favourite toppings on sesame-seed buns.

Per portion: 394 calories, 24.5 g protein, 17.3 g fat, 33.6 g carbohydrates, 1.5 mg dietary fibre, 65 mg calcium, 3.7 mg iron. Excellent source of iron.

MORDECAI RICHLER'S MEAT LOAF BURGER

Mordecai Richler's favourite burger has been adapted from his family's meat loaf recipe.

Makes 6 burgers

2 tsp	olive oil
1 stalk	celery, finely chopped (about ⅓ cup)
1	carrot, finely chopped (about ⅓ cup)
1 tbsp	finely chopped shallots
2	garlic cloves, minced
1	egg, lightly beaten
½ cup	crushed cornflakes
3 tbsp	chili sauce
2 tbsp	finely chopped Italian parsley
½ lb	ground pork
½ lb	ground veal
½ lb	ground beef
1 tsp each	salt and pepper
6	toasted hamburger buns

1. Heat olive oil in a small frying pan over medium-low heat. When oil is hot, add celery, carrot, shallots and garlic. Cook, stirring occasionally, until the vegetables are tender, about 10 minutes. Put in a large bowl, along with egg, cornflakes, chili sauce and parsley. Stir together until well combined. Add the meat, salt and pepper using your hands or a spoon, mix until well combined. Form into six patties.
2. Barbecue burgers for 5 to 7 minutes per side, or until cooked through. Serve in toasted hamburger buns with your favourite toppings.

Per portion: 465 calories, 27.6 g protein, 19 g fat, 44.6 g carbohydrates, 2.5 mg dietary fibre, 73 mg calcium, 4.4 mg iron. Excellent source of iron. Moderate in dietary fibre.

If you decide to revert to meat loaf, make the mixture as described, then roll the meat mixture around two softly boiled eggs, forming a meat loaf shape. Bake on a lightly greased baking sheet in a preheated 350F oven for 1 to 1 1/4 hours.

BRYAN ADAMS'S
FAVOURITE CAPERS CAFÉ VEGGIE BURGER

Bryan Adams's favourite burger comes from a restaurant called Capers Café, in his hometown of West Vancouver.

Makes 4 burgers

4 medium	carrots
1 small	beet
¾ cup	unsalted mixed nuts
1 tbsp	light sesame oil
2 tbsp	finely chopped onion
3 oz	crumbled tofu (preferably soft), about ¾ cup
⅓ cup	finely chopped mixed sprouts (bean, alfalfa, pea)
2 tsp	liquid honey
1 tbsp	miso
2	garlic cloves, minced
2 tsp	sesame seeds, preferably black
	Pinch of salt and freshly ground black pepper
⅓ to ½ cup	bread crumbs
2 tsp	vegetable oil

1. Using a food processor, finely process raw carrots until they resemble pulp. Measure out 1 cup and place in a medium-sized bowl. Finely process raw beet until it resembles pulp. Measure out 2 tablespoons and place in bowl with carrots. Process nuts until they are finely ground but with some texture still remaining. Measure out ¾ cup and add to the carrot mixture.
2. Heat 1 teaspoon sesame oil in a small frying pan over medium-low heat. Add onion and cook for 3 to 4 minutes, or just until onion has softened slightly.
3. Add the remaining 2 teaspoons sesame oil, onion mixture, tofu, sprouts, honey, miso, garlic, sesame seeds, salt and pepper to the carrot mixture. Stir until well mixed. Stir in ⅓ cup bread crumbs. If necessary, add a couple more tablespoons bread crumbs, until mixture is firm enough to hold its shape.
4. Form mixture into four burgers. This burger will fall apart on a BBQ unless you have a solid grill to prevent it falling through to the coals. Heat vegetable oil in a large non-stick skillet over medium heat. Place the burgers in the skillet and cook for 4 to 5 minutes a side, or until golden on the outside and hot inside.

 TIPS If you have a vegetable juicer, save the carrot or beet pulp left when you make juice and use it to make the burgers.

ELVIS STOJKO'S MOM'S BURGER

Canada's favourite ice-skating champion told us that his favourite burger was "created by my mother and is the very best I've ever tasted. But then, everything my mother cooks is the very best."

Makes 4 burgers

1 lb	lean ground beef
1	egg, lightly beaten
1	onion, finely chopped
⅓ cup	finely chopped Italian parsley
	Salt and freshly ground black pepper
4	hamburger buns, lightly toasted

1. In a medium-sized bowl, using your hands or a fork, combine beef, egg, onion, parsley, salt and pepper until well blended. Form into four burgers.
2. Barbecue for 4 to 5 minutes a side. Split the buns in half and fill with the burgers. Serve with your favourite burger toppings.

CAMILLA SCOTT'S CAJUN BURGERS

Camilla Scott, TV personality and former star of Mirvish Productions' *Crazy For You,* is crazy for burgers, especially this one made by her *What's For Dinner?* cooking show host buddy, Ken Kostick.

Makes 8 burgers

2 lbs	lean ground beef, turkey or chicken, or a combination
½ cup	finely chopped green pepper
½ cup	finely chopped red pepper
1	tomato, finely chopped
1 small	onion, finely chopped
1	garlic clove, minced
1	egg
½ cup	finely chopped coriander
1 tsp	finely chopped jalapeño pepper
½ tsp each	paprika, salt and pepper
8	buns

1. Preheat grill to medium-high heat. In a large bowl, combine all the burger ingredients, and mix well. Divide into eight equal portions and shape each portion into a patty.
2. Place the burgers on a well-greased grill and cook each side for 4 to 5 minutes, or until cooked through. Serve in buns.

Per serving: 373 calories, 26.3 g protein, 13.8 g fat, 34.5 g carbohydrates, 1.8 mg dietary fibre, 61 mg calcium, 3.8 mg iron, 35 mcg folacin. Excellent source of vitamin B12, iron and zinc. Good source of vitamin C and vitamin B6.

TIPS You can substitute 1/4 cup low-fat yogurt for the egg.

THE WEALTHY BARBER'S BURGER ALARM

David Chilton, author of one of Canada's all-time bestsellers, *The Wealthy Barber,* is also publisher of *Looneyspoons,* a low-fat cookbook by Janet and Greta Podleski that's made fun with puns and jokes. Here, David shares his favourite looney, yet lean, burger with us.

Makes 4 burgers

½ lb	extra-lean ground beef
½ lb	lean ground turkey
2 tbsp	minced onion
2	garlic cloves, minced
1	egg white
1 tbsp	ketchup
1 tsp	Worcestershire sauce
1 tsp each	chili powder and celery seeds
½ tsp each	ground cumin, salt and black pepper
4	buns

1. Preheat grill to medium-high heat. In a large bowl, combine all the burger ingredients and mix well. Divide mixture into four equal portions and shape each into a patty.
2. Place burgers on a well-greased grill and cook each side for 4 to 5 minutes, or until cooked through. Served in buns, topped with your favourite garnishes.

Per serving: 387 calories, 27.7 g protein, 14.7 g fat, 34.5 g carbohydrates, 1.5 mg dietary fibre, 71 mg calcium, 3.6 mg iron, 29 mcg folacin. Excellent source of vitamin B12, iron and zinc. Good source of vitamin B6.

WEI CHEN'S LAMB BURGERS

Wei Chen, news anchor at CTV, likes to top her lamb burgers with tzatziki for a sun-kissed taste of Greece. Wei often substitutes leftover cooked couscous for the bread crumbs.

Makes 4 burgers

1 lb	ground lamb
½ cup	bread crumbs
¼ cup	finely chopped fresh mint, fresh basil or parsley
1	garlic clove, minced
½ tsp	ground cumin
¼ tsp	ground coriander
¼ tsp	turmeric
¼ tsp	cayenne (optional)
¼ tsp	salt
1	egg
4	pita pockets
	Tzatziki (optional)
	Toppings: chopped red onion, chopped tomatoes and shredded lettuce

1. Preheat grill to medium-high heat. In a large bowl, combine all the burger ingredients and mix well. Divide mixture into four equal portions and shape each into a patty.
2. Place the burgers on a well-greased grill and cook each side for 4 to 5 minutes, or until cooked through. Serve in pita pockets, top with tzatziki sauce and toppings.

Per serving: 454 calories, 27.1 g protein, 20.2 g fat, 38.6 g carbohydrates, 0.5 g dietary fibre, 88 mg calcium, 4.1 mg iron, 61 mcg folacin. Excellent source of vitamin B12, iron and zinc.

Tzatziki is a delicious Greek yogurt, cucumber and garlic dip available in the dairy or deli section of many supermarkets.

NANCY SAKOVICH'S ALIEN BURGER

Nancy Sakovich, of TV's *PSI Factor*, brings us this recipe via outer space. A few years ago, her uncle was abducted by vegetarian aliens and this is what he claims they fed him. No surprise that this veggie burger tastes out of this world.

Makes 4 burgers

2 tbsp	olive oil
1	onion, finely chopped
2	carrots, grated
1 stalk	celery, finely chopped
2	garlic cloves, minced
1	19-oz can green or brown lentils, drained and rinsed
½ tsp each	ground cumin and coriander seed
⅓ cup	chopped parsley
1 tbsp	lemon juice
½ cup	quick-cooking oats
⅓ cup	hulled sunflower seeds
¼ cup	whole wheat flour or unbleached white flour
	Salt and pepper to taste
4	buns, preferably whole wheat

1. Heat 1 tablespoon oil in a large frying pan over medium heat. Add onion, carrots, celery and garlic. Stir until lightly browned, about 10 minutes; add lentils, spices, parsley and lemon juice; stir to blend. Remove from heat.
2. Mash lentils until smooth using the back of a spoon. Stir in oats, sunflower seeds and flour. Add salt and pepper.
3. With flour-covered hands, shape the mixture into four patties. Heat the remaining oil in a clean non-stick frying pan, over medium heat. Cook each side for 3 to 5 minutes or until browned, crisp and hot throughout. Serve with your favourite toppings.

Per serving: 506 calories, 21.8 g protein, 15.9 g fat, 75.7 g carbohydrates, 13.7 mg dietary fibre, 138 mg calcium, 7.3 mg iron, 263 mcg folacin. Excellent source of vitamin A, vitamin B6, iron and zinc. Contains very high amount of dietary fibre.

TIPS For a spicy burger, add hot sauce to the mixture.

CHARMAINE CROOKS'S
CHICKEN AND VEGGIE BURGER

Vancouverite Charmaine Crooks is a Canadian Championship gold medalist in track, Olympic silver medalist in the 4-by-400-m relay, and the only Canadian woman to break the two-minute barrier in the 800 metres. Charmaine's burger recipe is quick and easy to prepare, nutritious and delicious.

Makes 4 burgers

1 lb	ground chicken
1	egg, lightly beaten
2 tbsp	dry bread crumbs
	Salt and black pepper
1 small	zucchini, cut lengthwise into thin strips
	Olive oil
8 slices	sourdough bread
2	garlic cloves, sliced
	Light mayonnaise
2	fresh plum tomatoes, sliced
	Lettuce
	About 8 fresh basil leaves

1.   Preheat barbecue to medium. In a medium-sized bowl, combine chicken, egg, bread crumbs, salt and pepper. Form into four patties. Place the patties on the greased grill and barbecue for 5 to 8 minutes per side, until the burgers are cooked through. Meanwhile, brush zucchini strips lightly with oil and sprinkle with salt and pepper. Place zucchini strips on grill; they'll take about 2 minutes per side.
2.   Lightly brush slices of bread with oil and barbecue for about 30 seconds a side until hot.
3.   Remove bread, burgers and zucchini from barbecue. Rub bread with the cut side of garlic, then spread lightly with mayonnaise. Top with tomatoes, lettuce and basil leaves.

Per serving: 448 calories, 29.3 g protein, 18 g fat, 40.2 g carbohydrates, 2.1 mg dietary fibre, 34 mg calcium, 3.2 mg iron, 49 mcg folacin. Excellent source of zinc. Good source of vitamin B6, vitamin B12, folacin and iron. Moderate in dietary fibre.

KARYN MONK'S REBEL BURGERS

Karyn Monk's second novel, *The Rebel and the Redcoat* (Bantam), makes perfect summer reading to go with her savory Rebel Burgers.

Makes 4 burgers

1 lb	extra-lean ground beef
1	egg
1	garlic clove, minced
3 tbsp	barbecue sauce
1 tbsp	Dijon mustard
¼ tsp	Worcestershire sauce
½ tsp each	salt and black pepper
	Slices of cheddar cheese, lettuce, tomatoes, pickles, ketchup, mayonnaise, mustard and hot peppers
4	kaiser or onion buns

1. Preheat barbecue to medium-high. Combine beef, egg, garlic, barbecue sauce, Dijon, Worcestershire sauce, salt and pepper in a medium-sized bowl. Do not overmix or hamburgers will be tough. Form into four patties.
2. Place patties on greased grill and barbecue for 5 minutes per side, or until cooked through. Place cheese on burgers just before removing from barbecue. Serve, topped with all the "fixings," in toasted buns.

Per serving: 392 calories, 30.4 g protein, 11.7 g fat, 39.5 g carbohydrates, 1.9 mg dietary fibre, 53 mg calcium, 4.0 mg iron, 35 mcg folacin. Excellent source of vitamin B12 and iron. Good source of vitamin B6 and folacin.

PHIL GUERREO'S CLASSIC CANADIAN BURGER

Phil Guerreo, known for hosting YTV's *The Zone*, is one cool guy. His burger recipe is straightforward and downright delicious.

Makes 4 burgers

1 lb	medium-ground beef
2 tsp	Worcestershire sauce
1 small	onion, finely chopped
2	garlic cloves, minced
1	egg, lightly beaten
½ cup	dried bread crumbs
½ tsp	salt
	Pepper to taste
	Slices of cheddar cheese or Monterey Jack cheese
4	sesame-seed buns

1. Preheat barbecue to medium-high. In a medium-sized bowl, combine meat, Worcestershire sauce, onion, garlic, egg, bread crumbs, salt and pepper to taste. Do not overmix or hamburgers will be tough. Form into four patties.
2. Place on greased grill and barbecue for about 5 minutes per side, or until cooked through. Serve topped with cheese in toasted buns.

Per serving: 435 calories, 27.8 g protein, 17.4 g fat , 40 g carbohydrates, 1.7 mg dietary fibre, 77 mg calcium, 3.8 mg iron, 39 mcg folacin. Excellent source of vitamin B12, iron and zinc. Good source of vitamin B6 and folacin.

SHIRLEY SOLOMON'S BURGER

TV personality Shirley Solomon shares her burger recipe, which she enjoys with her husband, Les.

Makes 4 burgers

1 lb	lean ground beef
2 tbsp	ketchup
1 tbsp	mustard
2	egg whites or 1 egg, lightly beaten
¼ cup	bread crumbs
1 tbsp	Worcestershire sauce
1 tsp	garlic powder
	Generous pinch of salt and freshly ground black pepper
4	hamburger buns, toasted

1.   Using your hands or a fork, combine all the ingredients except buns in a medium-sized bowl, until well combined. Form into four burgers.

2.   Barbecue burgers for 4 to 5 minutes a side. Split the hamburger buns and place the burgers inside. Serve with your farvourite toppings.

CARLA COLLINS'S TURKEY BURGER

Comedian and television star Carla Collins must like Christmas in July — she dresses up this turkey burger with cranberry sauce.

Makes 4 burgers

1 lb	lean ground turkey
2 tbsp	chopped onion
1	garlic clove, minced
¼ cup	dried bread crumbs
1	egg, lightly beaten
¼ cup	chicken broth
1 tbsp	finely chopped parsley
¼ tsp	chili flakes
¼ tsp	ground sage or poultry seasoning
	Salt and freshly ground black pepper to taste
4	buns
	Lettuce, tomato, low-fat mayonnaise and cranberry sauce

1.   Preheat barbecue to medium-high heat. In a large bowl, mix turkey, onion, garlic, bread crumbs, egg, chicken broth and seasonings until well combined. Form into four patties.

2.   Place on a greased grill and barbecue for 5 to 8 minutes per side, or until burgers are cooked through. Split the buns and toast them if you wish. Top with lettuce, tomato, mayonnaise and cranberry sauce.

Per serving: 451 calories, 28.6 g protein, 19.6 g fat, 37.9 g carbohydrates, 1.5 mg dietary fibre, 88 mg calcium, 3.5 mg iron, 36 mcg folacin. Excellent source of iron and zinc. Good source of vitamin B6, vitamin B12 and folacin.

HERBIE KUHN'S STUFFED BURGER

Herbie Kuhn, the voice of the Toronto Raptors, gets involved — just like the basketball team members — by making time to speak with kids in an effort to steer them in the right direction.

Makes 4 burgers

1 lb	lean ground beef
¼ cup	beer
2	green onions, finely chopped
2 tbsp	dried bread crumbs
2 tbsp	finely chopped parsley
2 tbsp	salsa
	Salt and pepper to taste
4	½-inch pieces cheddar, mozzarella or Swiss cheese
4	toasted buns
	Mayonnaise and lettuce leaves

1. Preheat barbecue to medium-high. Combine beef, beer, onions, bread crumbs, parsley, salsa, and salt and pepper in a large bowl. Set aside. Shape one-quarter of the meat around one piece of cheese to enclose it, then shape it into a burger, making sure the cheese is thoroughly enclosed. Repeat with the remaining meat and cheese.
2. Place on greased grill and barbecue for 5 minutes per side, or until cooked through. Spread the buns with mayonnaise and place burgers in buns. Top with lettuce leaves and your favourite toppings.

Per serving: 384 calories, 26.3 g protein, 13.9 g fat , 36 g carbohydrates, 1.6 mg dietary fibre, 80 mg calcium, 3.9 mg iron, 35 mcg folacin. Excellent source of vitamin B12, iron and zinc. Good source of folacin.

"Hamburger Disease," as it is known, is caused by a strain of *E.coli* bacteria, which can be found in ground meats and foods such as raw milk, mayonnaise and unpasteurized juice, as well as uncleaned vegetables and water. Agriculture Canada recommends that ground meats be used within a day or two of being packaged. Freezing the food does not kill the bacteria, nor can it be detected through sight or smell. To avoid spreading bacteria, keep work areas clean and wash hands, utensils and counters after handling raw meat or poultry. The good news is that the bacteria is easily destroyed through proper cooking. Cook all burgers — poultry, beef, veal or pork — until well done.

NO-FUSS DESSERTS

Nothing tops dinner like a homemade dessert. The problem, of course, is that you just ran in from work at six and most nights, it's enough just to try to get a hot meal on the table — let alone dessert!

Well, here are 25 no-fuss desserts that can be assembled in minutes then popped in the oven to be served hot and steaming after dinner. Whether it's Easy-Bake Apple Betty or Quick Coffee Pie, these recipes are sure to delight you — and, of course, the dessert fiends in your family.

CREAMY COCONUT RICE PUDDING

Coconut adds a twist to this old-fashioned rice pudding.

Makes 4 cups

¾ cup	Italian-style (arborio) rice
1 ½ cups	water
	Pinch of salt
3 cups	milk
1	14-oz can coconut milk
½ cup	sweetened shredded coconut
⅓ cup	granulated sugar
1 tsp	ground ginger
1	egg yolk
1 tsp	vanilla

1.   Put rice, water and salt in a large saucepan. Bring to a boil, then reduce heat and simmer, uncovered, for 10 to 15 minutes until water is absorbed.
2.   Stir in milk, coconut milk, coconut, sugar and ginger. Bring to a boil, then reduce heat and simmer gently for 30 minutes, stirring occasionally until mixture is creamy.
3.   Put yolk in a small bowl. Stir about ½ cup of the hot rice mixture into yolk. Then stir the yolk mixture back into rice pudding. Stir in vanilla. Remove from heat and turn into a serving bowl. Serve the pudding warm or press a piece of clear wrap onto its surface; refrigerate until ready to serve. Serve as is, or sprinkle with toasted coconut.

Per half-cup: 227 calories, 5.8 g protein, 14.6 g fat, 31.9 g carbohydrates, 0.5 g dietary fibre, 124 mg calcium, 1.9 mg iron

Arborio rice is an Italian short-grain rice. It is found in supermarkets, Italian grocery stores and some bulk food stores. It is ideal for rice pudding because it absorbs lots of liquid without turning mushy and gives the pudding a creamy texture. Arborio rice is also used for one of Italy's most famous dishes — risotto.

SINFULLY DELICIOUS BAKED CUSTARD

Custard so good it's as smooth as silk.

Serves 6

1	orange
1 cup	whipping cream
1 cup	half-and-half cream
1	egg
3	egg yolks
½ cup	granulated sugar
1 tbsp	vanilla

1.   Preheat oven to 350F. Using a sharp knife, cut peel away from orange in wide strips, being careful not to remove any of the bitter white pith.
2.   Heat whipping cream, half-and-half cream and orange peel in a medium saucepan over medium heat, just until bubbles form around the edge of the pan — 8 to 10 minutes. Meanwhile, whisk egg and yolks with sugar and vanilla in a large bowl. Once the cream is hot, place a strainer over a medium-sized bowl and pour the cream through it. Discard the orange peel in strainer. Whisk hot cream very gradually into the egg mixture.
3.   For easy pouring, transfer the hot mixture to a measuring cup, then pour it into 6 ungreased 6-ounce custard cups. Set the custard cups in a baking dish. Pour very hot water into the baking dish until it reaches halfway up the sides of the custard cups. This will help cook the custard more evenly.
4.   Bake until a knife inserted in the centre of one of the custards comes out nearly clean — about 40 minutes. Serve warm or at room temperature, dusted with cinnamon if you wish.

Per portion: 302 calories, 4.6 g protein, 22.5 g fat, 20.6 g carbohydrates, 0 g dietary fibre, 89 mg calcium, 0.5 mg iron

Be sure to remove the custard from the water bath when the cooking is complete, otherwise it will keep cooking. The centre will still be a bit jiggly, but will firm a little while cooling.

OLD-FASHIONED LEMON PUDDING CAKE

This Lemon Pudding Cake has a wonderful tart-sweet flavor combination.

Serves 4

1 to 2	lemons (if small, use 2)
2	eggs, at room temperature
¾ cup	granulated sugar
¼ cup	all-purpose flour
1 tbsp	butter, melted
1 cup	milk
¼ tsp	salt

1. Preheat oven to 350F. Finely grate 1 tablespoon peel from lemon. Set aside. Squeeze out ¼ cup juice from lemon(s). Set aside.
2. Separate eggs, placing whites in a medium-sized bowl and yolks in a small bowl. Beat yolks lightly with a fork.
3. Using a fork, stir sugar with flour in a large mixing bowl until well blended. Then stir in lemon juice, peel, egg yolks, butter and milk.
4. Beat egg whites with salt until stiff but not dry. Gently fold the whites into the lemon mixture. Pour into an ungreased 6-cup casserole dish. Bake in the centre of the oven for 30 to 35 minutes, until topping is set and golden brown. Let stand for 5 to 10 minutes before serving. Serve warm.

Per portion: 270 calories, 6.1 g protein, 6.6 g fat, 47.9 g carbohydrates, 0.4 g dietary fibre, 92 mg calcium, 0.8 mg iron

For a change of pace, turn our Lemon Pudding Cake into a Coconut Lime version by substituting lime juice and peel for lemon juice and peel, and adding 1/4 cup of shredded coconut to the lime mixture.

QUICK COFFEE PIE

To make your own flavored coffee, add about ½ to 1 tsp of flavored extract, such as orange almond or peppermint, to ½ cup of brewed coffee.

Serves 8

1	170-g chocolate pudding and pie filling (not instant)
2 ½ cups	milk
½ cup	strong brewed coffee, preferably flavored
2 tbsp	flavored liqueur (coffee, orange, almond or peppermint)
1	170-g purchased chocolate wafer crumb pie crust
½ cup	whipping cream
2 tbsp	granulated sugar
2 tbsp	toasted slivered almonds or finely grated chocolate (optional)

1. Prepare pudding filling, using milk and coffee and following the package directions. Once the pudding has come to a boil and thickened, remove from heat and stir in liqueur.
2. Turn the pudding into the pie shell and carefully put it in the refrigerator to set for about 2 hours. Once the pie is set, whip cream with sugar until soft peaks form when the beaters are lifted. Swirl the whipped cream over top of the pie. Top with toasted slivered almonds or grated chocolate.

Per piece: 314 calories, 4.6 g protein, 15.3 g fat, 41.8 g carbohydrates, 1.1 g dietary fibre, 112 mg calcium, 1.3 mg iron, 4 mcg folacin

Mix and match your favourite flavors — try almond-flavored liqueur, coffee with either almond or chocolate liqueur, and toasted slivered almonds as a garnish.

INDIVIDUAL ICE CREAM TRUFFLE BOMBES

 These "bombes" are a great easy-to-cheat dessert — and they pack a taste explosion.

Serves 4

4 medium	scoops coffee, chocolate or vanilla ice cream
4 small	chocolate truffles (your favourite flavor)
2 tbsp	coffee, orange or almond liqueur (optional)
2 tbsp	chocolate-covered coffee beans, orange peel or toasted hazelnuts for garnish
8	fancy cookies

1. Scoop ice cream into 4 bowls. Make an indentation in each scoop, then push a truffle into each. Spoon liqueur over truffle. Sprinkle with garnish. Stand the cookies in the ice cream.

Per bombe: 241 calories, 3.4 g protein, 16.3 g fat, 27.7 g carbohydrates, 1.1 g dietary fibre, 87 mg calcium, 0.2 mg iron, 1 mcg folacin. Good source of vitamin B12.

 When buying the ice cream, truffles, liqueur and garnish, pick flavors that go well together. For example, coffee ice cream with a hazelnut truffle, coffee liqueur and either toasted hazelnuts or a chocolate-covered beans garnish makes a delicious combination. Chocolate ice cream tastes fabulous with a plain chocolate or orange truffle, orange liqueur and orange peel for garnish.

QUICK STRAWBERRY SAUCE FOR CAKE

 Dress up a purchased pound cake with this fast and fancy sauce.

Makes about 1 ¾ cups

1 tbsp	cornstarch
¼ cup	orange juice
1	300-g pkg unsweetened whole strawberries
¼ cup	pure strawberry jam

1. Dissolve cornstarch in orange juice. Put the mixture in a medium-sized saucepan with strawberries and jam. Heat and stir continuously until mixture

comes to a boil and thickens slightly. Reduce heat to low and simmer gently for 1 more minute.

2. To serve, slice a pound cake or angel cake. Arrange the slices on a plate. Drizzle the warm or room-temperature sauce over top. Spoon a dollop of yogurt onto the plate.

Per portion: 41 calories, 0.2 g protein, 0 g fat, 10.4 g carbohydrates, 0.6 g dietary fibre, 7 mg calcium, 0.3 mg iron, 7 mcg folacin

TROPICAL FRUIT MERINGUES

 The fresh fruit in this dessert makes it a healthier choice for your family.

Serves 4

¼ cup	plain yogurt
2 tbsp	granulated sugar
1 tbsp	finely chopped crystallized ginger or stem ginger in syrup, drained
1 tbsp	lime juice
½ tsp	finely grated lime peel
½ cup	whipping cream
½ tsp	vanilla
2 cups	fresh fruit (sliced strawberries, mangoes or oranges, raspberries or kiwis), preferably a combination
4	purchased meringue nests
2 tbsp	sweetened flaked coconut, preferably toasted

1. Stir yogurt, sugar, ginger, lime juice and lime peel together; set aside. Whip cream with vanilla until soft peaks form. Beat cream into the yogurt mixture.
2. Spoon fruit into meringue nests. Top with the cream mixture. Sprinkle with toasted coconut. Serve immediately.

Per meringue: 288 calories, 3.2 g protein, 12.3 g fat, 44.7 g carbohydrates, 3.1 g dietary fibre, 74 mg calcium, 1.1 mg iron, 6 mcg folacin. Excellent source of vitamin A and vitamin C. Moderate in dietary fibre.

BANANA COFFEE CAKE

Your kids will go ape over this delightfully easy recipe.

Makes 1 cake

1 cup	well-mashed bananas (2 to 3)
½ cup	sour cream
2 tbsp	hot water
2 tbsp	instant coffee granules
2 ¼ cups	cake and pastry flour
1 tsp	brown sugar
1 tsp each	salt and cinnamon
½ tsp	ground nutmeg
½ cup	butter, at room temperature
1 ⅓ cups	granulated sugar
	Finely grated peel of 1 orange
2	eggs
1 tsp	vanilla extract
	Icing sugar (optional)

1. Preheat oven to 350F. Lightly butter a 9 x 13-inch baking pan. In a medium bowl, stir bananas with sour cream. Stir water with coffee until the granules are dissolved, and add to the banana mixture.

2. In a separate bowl, sift flour with brown sugar, salt, cinnamon and nutmeg. In a large bowl, beat butter with sugar and orange peel until light and fluffy. Beat in eggs one at a time until well blended. Beat in vanilla. Gradually beat in the flour mixture, alternating with the banana mixture, beginning and ending with flour.

3. Turn the mixture into the prepared pan and bake for 35 to 45 minutes, or until a cake tester inserted in the centre comes out clean. Cool in the pan on a rack for 10 minutes, then turn the cake onto the rack to cool completely. Dust lightly with icing sugar. This cake can be frozen.

Per piece: 119 calories, 1.5 g protein, 4.4 g fat, 18.9 g carbohydrates, 0.6 g dietary fibre, 114 mg calcium, 1.3 mg iron, 16 mcg folacin

Prepare a 400-g banana walnut cake mix according to the package directions, dissolving 1 tablespoon instant coffee granules into the water. Stir in the grated peel of 1 orange, 1 teaspoon cinnamon and 1/2 teaspoon ground nutmeg.

ESPRESSO BROWNIES

Make these brownies on the weekend and delight in your family's smiles all week long.

Makes 25

½ cup	butter
3 oz	unsweetened chocolate, chopped
2 tsp	instant espresso or coffee granules
1 ¼ cups	granulated sugar
2	eggs
1 tsp	vanilla
⅔ cup	all-purpose flour
½ tsp	salt
½ cup	coarsely chopped pecans, preferably toasted
½ cup	coarsely chopped bittersweet chocolate or chocolate chips

1. Preheat oven to 350F. Lightly butter and flour a 9-inch square baking pan. In a large saucepan over medium-low heat, stir butter with chocolate and espresso granules until butter and chocolate are melted and espresso granules are dissolved. Whisk in sugar, eggs and vanilla until blended. Stir in flour and salt until combined. Stir in pecans and chocolate.

2. Pour into the prepared pan and smooth the top. Bake for 25 to 30 minutes, or until a cake tester inserted in centre comes out nearly clean but with some moist crumbs attached. Cool completely in the pan on a rack. Cut when cooled.

Per square: 139 calories, 1.7 g protein, 8.9 g fat, 15.6 g carbohydrates,
1.1 g dietary fibre, 10 mg calcium, 0.7 mg iron, 4 mcg folacin

 Brownies can be stored in an airtight container or frozen.

VERY BERRY CHERRY COBBLER

Make this cobbler once and it will become a seasonal favourite.

Serves 10

4 cups	strawberries, halved
2 cups	sweet cherries, pitted
1 cup	raspberries
1 cup	blueberries
⅓ cup each	granulated sugar and cornstarch
1 to 1 ¼	cups all-purpose flour
1 tsp	baking powder
	Finely grated peel of 1 lemon
	Generous pinch of salt
⅓ cup	butter, cut into pieces
⅓ cup	milk

1.   Preheat oven to 350F. Cut strawberries into quarters if they're large. Put the fruit in a large bowl. Stir sugar and cornstarch together, then toss with the fruit until combined. Turn the fruit into a 10-inch baking dish.

2.   In a separate bowl, stir 1 cup flour with baking powder, lemon peel and salt until combined. Cut in butter until the mixture is crumbly. Using a fork, gradually stir in milk just until it is combined (do not overmix). If the dough is sticky, add a bit more flour. Gather the dough into a ball and knead it a couple of times on a lightly floured surface. Roll it into a piece large enough to cover the fruit, allowing an extra ½-inch all the way around. Tuck the overlapping dough under the edges. Cut three small slits in the pastry. Set the dish on a baking sheet to catch the drips.

3.   Bake, uncovered, for 45 to 50 minutes, or until topping is golden brown and juices from fruit are bubbling around the edges. Let stand for about 15 minutes before serving.

Per serving: 199 calories, 2.6 g protein, 7.1 g fat, 33.1 g carbohydrates, 3 g dietary fibre, 42 mg calcium, 1 mg iron, 11 mcg folacin. Excellent source of vitamin C and good source of vitamin B6. Moderate in dietary fibre.

When you have a lot of cherries to pit, use a cherry pitter. They don't cost a fortune, and they make the job a lot easier.

QUICK FRUIT GRANOLA CRUMBLE

Fresh fruit and low-fat granola combine to make a too-good-to-be-true dessert.

Serves 8

8	unpeeled nectarines, pitted and sliced
5	unpeeled apricots or plums, pitted and sliced
½ cup	granulated sugar
¼ tsp	almond extract
1 ½ cups	purchased granola (low-fat or regular)
¼ cup	all-purpose flour
¼ cup	butter, cut into pieces

1. Preheat oven to 350F. In a large bowl, toss together nectarines, apricots (or plums), sugar and almond extract. Turn the mixture into a 9-inch baking dish.
2. In a separate bowl, stir granola with flour. Cut in butter, trying to keep granola chunky. Sprinkle the mixture over the fruit. Bake, uncovered, for 45 to 55 minutes, until fruit is hot and tender. If the topping browns too quickly, cover it loosely with foil.

Per serving: 262 calories, 3.9 g protein, 8 g fat , 46.3 g carbohydrates, 3.7 g dietary fibre, 32 mg calcium, 1.0 mg iron, 4 mcg folacin. Good source of vitamin A. Moderate in dietary fibre.

CHOCOLATE PECAN PIE

Why not make any weekday really special with this truly decadent pie?

Serves 10

1	9-inch frozen pie shell
½ cup	granulated sugar
⅔ cup	corn syrup
⅓ cup	chopped unsweetened chocolate (about 2 squares)
2 tbsp	butter, at room temperature
2	eggs
½ tsp	vanilla
	Pinch of salt
½ cup	coarsely chopped pecans
¾ cup	pecan halves

1.   Preheat oven to 400F. Thaw pie shell for 10 minutes. Prick it all over with the tines of a fork. Bake it for 8 to 10 minutes, until golden. Meanwhile, in a small saucepan stir sugar with corn syrup until they are dissolved. Remove from heat; stir in chopped chocolate and butter until they are dissolved. Remove pie shell from the oven and reduce the oven temperature to 350F.

2.   In a separate bowl, beat eggs with the vanilla and salt. Stir them into the sugar mixture until blended. Sprinkle chopped pecans over the bottom of the warm pie shell. Top with the chocolate mixture. Sprinkle evenly with pecan halves. Bake in the preheated oven for about 20 minutes, or just until filling appears set. Let stand at room temperature. Serve at room temperature with whipping cream if you wish.

Per portion: 351 calories, 4.1 g protein, 21.9 g fat, 38.7 g carbohydrates, 2.1 g dietary fibre, 28 mg calcium, 2.1 mg iron. Good source of iron and contains a moderate amount of dietary fibre.

To store, cover pie at room temperature. It will stay fresh for a couple of days. To freeze, cool completely and wrap well before freezing. If you make your own pastry, prebake the shell before filling it to ensure the crust is baked.

SOUR CREAM RHUBARB PIE

MW READER RECIPE: This Reader Recipe was inspired by a recipe sent to us by Carole Divell of Caledon, Ontario. She got it from a neighbor 10 years earlier and has been making it ever since. Carole says the pie is best eaten within a day or two, if it lasts that long!

Serves 10

	Pastry for 9-inch deep-dish pie, or a frozen deep-dish pie shell
4 cups	cubed rhubarb (½-inch cubes)
1 cup	granulated sugar
⅓ cup	all-purpose flour
½ cup	sour cream

Topping

½ cup	all-purpose flour
½ cup	brown sugar
¼ cup	butter, at room temperature

1. Preheat oven to 450F. Line 9-inch pie plate with pastry. Or thaw frozen pie shell according to package directions. Toss rhubarb with sugar, flour and sour cream. Turn the mixture into pie shell.
2. Use your fingertips to blend the topping ingredients together until crumbly. Sprinkle over the top of the pie filling.
3. Bake for 15 minutes. Reduce the temperature to 350F and continue to bake for 35 to 40 minutes, or until fruit is tender, filling is set and crumbs are brown. Let stand for 20 minutes before serving.

Per serving: 314 calories, 3 g protein, 12.4 g fat, 48.9 g carbohydrates, 1.5 g dietary fibre, 67 mg calcium, 1.2 mg iron

BANANA BREAD

MW READER RECIPE: Sandra Sullivan of Toronto sent her favourite recipe for banana bread. It's easy to prepare and a great way to use overripe bananas. This bread can be made anytime and frozen.

Makes 12 slices

1 ½ cups	all-purpose flour
1 tsp	baking soda
½ tsp	salt
½ cup	butter, at room temperature
1 cup	granulated sugar
2	eggs
3 medium	overripe bananas, mashed
½ cup	chopped walnuts (optional)

1.   Preheat oven to 350F and lightly grease a 9 x 5 x 3-inch loaf pan. In a small bowl, stir together flour, baking soda and salt. In a large bowl, using an electric mixer, beat butter with sugar until light and fluffy. Beat in eggs until combined. Use a spoon to stir in flour mixture, mashed bananas and walnuts until combined.

2.   Spoon the batter into the prepared loaf pan, smoothing the top. Bake for 50 to 60 minutes, or until a cake tester (or a knife) inserted in the centre of the loaf comes out clean. If the loaf begins to turn dark, cover it loosely with a piece of foil. Cool on a rack, then serve. Banana bread will keep well for several days when tightly wrapped.

Per serving: 227 calories, 3 g protein, 8.8 g fat, 35.2 g carbohydrates,
1 g dietary fibre, 11 mg calcium, 0.9 mg iron

APPLE STRUDEL

Ready-made phyllo pastry takes most of the fuss out of making this great strudel.

Makes 11 pieces

6 medium	apples, peeled, cored and cut into ¼-inch slices
2 tbsp	butter
⅓ cup	brown sugar
¼ tsp each	ground nutmeg and ground cardamom (optional)
	Finely grated peel of 1 lemon
1 tbsp	lemon juice
¼ cup each	raisins and chopped almonds or hazelnuts
6 sheets	phyllo pastry
¼ to ⅓ cup	warm melted butter
½ tbsp	dry bread crumbs
	Icing sugar (optional)

1.   Put apples, butter, brown sugar, nutmeg, cardamom, lemon peel, lemon juice and raisins in a large wide skillet. Cover and cook over medium heat, stirring occasionally, for 8 to 10 minutes, or until apples are slightly tender. Remove the cover and continue to cook, stirring occasionally, until apples are tender and juices have evaporated — 5 to 8 minutes. Stir in nuts. Cool the filling.
2.   Place one sheet of the phyllo on the counter; brush it with the melted butter. Place another sheet on top; line up the edges and brush the second sheet with butter. Repeat with remaining sheets. Sprinkle the last buttered sheet with the bread crumbs.
3.   Preheat oven to 375F. Lightly grease a baking sheet. Place the filling in a 2-inch-wide strip 1 ½ inches from the bottom of the long edge of phyllo, leaving 1 ½ inches of phyllo at either end. Fold both ends of phyllo over filling. Roll phyllo tightly around filling, like a jelly roll, making sure the ends are tucked in to prevent leaking. Using a sharp knife, cut the phyllo nearly through to the apple mixture to mark serving sizes. Bake for about 25 minutes until golden brown and crisp. Cool on the baking sheet. When cool, dust with icing sugar and cut into slices. Serve with ice cream or whipped cream.

Per serving: 43 calories, 1.4 g protein, 1.7 g fat, 5.5 g carbohydrates, 0.3 g dietary fibre, 19 mg calcium, 0.3 mg iron. Moderate in dietary fibre.

While working with phyllo, prevent it from drying out by keeping it covered with waxed paper or a barely moist tea towel. When brushing the phyllo with butter, begin at the outside edges, as these are quicker to dry out.

SUGAR PIE

Originally made with locally produced maple sugar, this Quebecois specialty is now frequently made with brown sugar. It's not quite the same as the original, but the results are delicious. One thing's for sure: this is a pie for a sweet tooth.

Serves 10

2 cups	brown sugar
1 ¼ cups	all-purpose flour
½ cup	whipping cream
1	egg
1 tbsp	corn syrup
1 tsp	vanilla
¾ cup	coarsely chopped pecans (optional)
	9-inch prebaked pie crust

1. Preheat oven to 350F. Stir brown sugar with flour in a medium-sized bowl until mixed. In a separate bowl, whisk cream with egg, corn syrup and vanilla until blended. Gradually whisk the cream mixture into the brown sugar mixture until it's well blended and there are no lumps. Stir in nuts if using. The mixture will be quite thick.
2. Set prebaked pie crust on a cookie sheet. Turn the filling into the pie crust. Bake on the bottom shelf of the oven for 40 to 50 minutes or until filling is set and golden brown. Serve warm or at room temperature with a scoop of vanilla ice cream.

Per serving: 365 calories, 3.6 g protein, 10.9 g fat, 64.3 g carbohydrates, 0.9 g dietary fibre, 54 mg calcium, 2.1 mg iron

If using a purchased pie shell, make sure to buy a deep-dish 9-inch shell.

TRIPLE CHOCOLATE CHEESECAKE

This dessert is a chocolate lover's dream-come-true.

Serves 14

Crust

1 ¾ cups	chocolate wafer crumbs
⅓ cup	melted butter
½ cup	finely chopped milk chocolate

Filling

20 oz	cream cheese, at room temperature
1 cup	granulated sugar
3	eggs, lightly beaten
3 tbsp	coffee liqueur
1 cup	sour cream
6 oz	bittersweet chocolate, melted

Topping

4 oz	white chocolate, finely chopped
3 tbsp	whipping cream
	Cocoa for dusting (optional)

1.   Stir crust ingredients together in a medium-sized bowl until blended. Press into the bottom and partway up the sides of a greased 9 ½-inch springform pan. Refrigerate.

2.   Preheat oven to 325F. In a large mixing bowl, beat cream cheese with sugar until well combined. Beat in eggs one at a time, beating well after each addition. Beat in liqueur, sour cream and chocolate. Pour the filling into the base. Bake for 45 minutes, or until the centre is barely firm. Turn off the oven, leaving the cheesecake inside with the door slightly ajar for 1 hour. Cool on a rack.

3.   In the top of a double boiler set over hot water, stir white chocolate and cream until chocolate is melted and smooth. Scrape chocolate onto the centre of the cooled cheesecake and carefully spread to cover. Refrigerate overnight. Dust with cocoa just before serving.

Per portion: 506 calories, 8.3 g protein, 36.7 g fat, 40.9 g carbohydrates, 0.9 g dietary fibre, 105 mg calcium, 2.3 mg iron

NO-BAKE KEY LIME CHEESECAKE

MW READER RECIPE: Penny Degeer of Toronto created her Key Lime Cheesecake as a surprise treat for her younger brother. Penny decorates the cheesecake with lime slices and whipping cream.

Serves 12

Crust

1 ⅓ cups	graham cracker crumbs
¼ cup	granulated sugar
⅓ cup	melted butter

Filling

1 ¼ cups	lime juice, either bottled or fresh
¼ cup	water
2 envelopes	unflavored gelatin
1 ½ cups	granulated sugar
5	eggs, lightly beaten
½ cup	butter, at room temperature
2	8-oz pkgs cream cheese, at room temperature
½ cup	whipping cream

1.   In a medium-sized bowl, stir together crust ingredients. Press into the bottom of a 9-inch springform pan. Refrigerate.

2.   Stir lime juice with water in a medium-sized saucepan. Sprinkle gelatin over the mixture; let it stand for 5 minutes. Stir in sugar and eggs. Place the mixture over medium heat; stir continuously until mixture thickens and just comes to a boil — 5 to 7 minutes (it may appear to be separated). If necessary, strain out any bits of egg white.

3.   In a large mixing bowl, beat butter with cream cheese, scraping the sides of the bowl often, until well combined. Beat in the hot lime mixture and continue to mix until blended. Refrigerate until slightly firm, stirring every 20 minutes, for a total of 40 minutes.

4.   Beat cream until stiff peaks form; fold it into the lime mixture. Pour the filling into the prepared crust and refrigerate overnight.

Per portion: 490 calories, 8.1 g protein, 34.1 g fat, 41.1 g carbohydrates, 0.3 g dietary fibre, 62 mg calcium, 1.3 mg iron

APPLESAUCE PIE

MW READER RECIPE: Wilma Cassidy of Toronto sent us her 91-year-old mother's recipe for this applesauce pie, a family favourite during apple harvest every September. It's not too sweet and makes a nice change from traditional apple pie.

Serves 8

Filling

⅓ cup	butter, at room temperature
⅓ cup	granulated sugar
3	egg yolks
2 cups	thick applesauce (homemade or purchased), preferably unsweetened
1 tbsp	lemon juice
½ tsp	cinnamon
¼ tsp	nutmeg
1	9-inch partially baked pie crust, at room temperature

Topping

3	egg whites, at room temperature
¼ cup	granulated sugar

1. Preheat oven to 350F. Using an electric mixer, beat butter with sugar until light and fluffy. Beat in egg yolks, then applesauce, lemon juice, cinnamon and nutmeg until thoroughly blended (mixture may appear curdled). Pour the mixture into the pie shell, smoothing the top. Bake on the bottom shelf of the oven for 50 to 55 minutes. Filling will firm upon cooling.
2. To make the topping, beat egg whites on high speed just until foamy. Gradually add sugar, beating until stiff peaks form. Top cooled pie filling with meringue topping, spreading it right to the edges of the pastry crust. Use the back of a spoon to make swirls in meringue.
3. Return the pie to preheated 350F oven; bake until the meringue has browned slightly, 13 to 15 minutes. Cool on a rack. Serve at room temperature.

Per portion: 293 calories, 4.0 g protein, 17.3 g fat, 31.7 g carbohydrates, 1.2 g dietary fibre, 18 mg calcium, 0.9 mg iron

EASY-BAKE APPLE BETTY

 quick & **EASY**

MW READER RECIPE: Kathleen Fawcett of Thunder Bay, Ontario, gets credit for this couldn't-be-easier Apple Betty. As she says, "Serve it and pretend you've slaved for hours. No one said *great* couldn't be *easy* too!" We've adapted it slightly so there's enough (and then some) for the whole family.

Makes 20 pieces

2	19-oz cans apple pie filling
1	500-g spice cake mix
⅓ cup	melted butter

1. Preheat oven to 350F. Butter a 13 x 9-inch baking pan and spread pie filling evenly over the base of the pan.
2. Prepare cake according to package directions. Carefully and evenly, spread the cake batter over the pie filling. Drizzle melted butter over the cake batter. Bake for 40 to 45 minutes, or until golden brown and a cake tester inserted in the centre of the cake comes out clean. Cool on a rack until warm. To serve, cut the cake and invert it onto a plate. Serve with whipped cream if you wish.

Per portion: 243 calories, 2.1 g protein, 11.1 g fat, 34.5 g carbohydrates, 1 g dietary fibre, 27 mg calcium, 0.5 mg iron

ESPRESSO BROWNIE ICE CREAM PIE

For lovers of strong coffee and chocolate.

Serves 8

1 tsp	instant coffee powder
1	450-g pkg brownie mix
1 tsp	cinnamon
¼ cup	chocolate fudge sauce
1 to 2 tbsp	coffee-flavored liqueur (optional)
1	container of 500-g coffee or chocolate ice cream
Garnish	cinnamon sticks, chocolate-covered espresso beans

1. Grease a 9-inch pie plate. Dissolve coffee powder in 2 teaspoons hot water; set aside. Prepare brownies according to package directions, stirring cinnamon

and coffee mixture into brownie mix. Bake according to the package directions for an 8-inch pan. Leave brownies in the pie plate to cool on a wire rack.

2. Stir coffee-flavored liqueur (if using) into chocolate sauce. To serve, spoon chocolate sauce over individual dessert plates. Cut cooled brownie into wedges and place on chocolate sauce on dessert plate. Scoop coffee ice cream onto brownie. Garnish each with a couple of cinnamon sticks and a few espresso beans.

Per portion: 497 calories, 5.8 g protein, 26.9 g fat, 63.1 g carbohydrates, 0.4 g dietary fibre, 125 mg calcium, 1.4 mg iron

Brownies and sauce can be prepared in advance. Chocolate-covered espresso beans are available at specialty coffee shops.

CHOCOLATE FONDUE

Chocolate fondue can be assembled in minutes for great family fun gathering around the fondue pot.

Serves 10

6 oz	bittersweet chocolate, finely chopped
4 oz	semisweet chocolate, finely chopped
1 cup	whipping cream
¼ cup	corn syrup
1 tsp	vanilla
	Strawberries, pineapple, apple, kiwi and banana chunks, orange segments, cubes of pound cake or angel food cake, pieces of candied ginger for dipping

1. Put chopped chocolate, cream and corn syrup into the fondue pot. Cook the mixture on the stovetop over low heat, stirring frequently until the chocolate has melted and the mixture is smooth. Remove from heat, and stir in vanilla. Place the fondue pot over its base; serve the sauce warm with assorted dipping fruit and cubes of cake.

Per portion (sauce only): 242 calories, 2.3 g protein, 19.2 g fat, 21.4 g carbohydrates, 1.8 g dietary fibre, 33 mg calcium, 1.6 mg iron.

This fondue recipe can easily be cut in half. It can also be prepared in advance and refrigerated, then reheated over low heat just before serving.

CHOCOLATE CARAMEL SAUCE

Serve over ice cream for an easy mid-week treat.

Makes 1 cup

½ cup	whipping cream
20	caramels, unwrapped
1 tsp	coffee granules (optional)
3 oz	bittersweet chocolate, chopped

1.   Heat cream with caramels and coffee granules (if using) in a small saucepan, over medium heat, stirring occasionally. When caramels have melted, remove the saucepan from the heat and stir in chocolate until smooth. Serve warm or at room temperature.

Per portion: 85 calories, 0.9 g protein, 5.6 g fat, 9.4 g carbohydrates, 0.3 g dietary fibre, 22 mg calcium, 0.4 mg iron

To unwrap caramels more easily, put them in the freezer for about 10 minutes.

THE GREAT CANADIAN COOKIE SWAP

The Great Canadian Cookie Swap debuted in 1993 and has become a popular annual feature in the magazine. It all began when Peggy Mowry of Darwell, Alberta, wrote to us to tell us about her traditional cookie swap. "Ten years ago," wrote Peggy, "I had a brainstorm that I thought would save me a lot of time baking Christmas cookies and bars. I don't mind baking a batch of cookies, but I sure get tired of all the mess it takes to bake a variety. So I invited 10 of my friends to come to my house for lunch. I told them I would treat them to my special Old-Fashioned New England Clam Chowder in exchange for a dozen of their special Christmas cookies or goodies.

From that small gathering of women in Darwell, *MW* has invited the whole country to take part in our cookie swap. It was next to impossible to pick just 25 cookies and bars from five years of amazing Reader Recipes, but here they are — the best of the best!

THE ULTIMATE CHOCOLATE BROWNIE COOKIE

MW READER RECIPE: Marilyn Turpin of Dorval, Quebec, sent us this recipe from her family's favourites. No wonder! These are a chocolate lover's heaven.

Makes 4 ½ dozen

1 ⅓ cups	butter or margarine
1 cup	granulated sugar
⅔ cup	brown sugar
2	eggs, lightly beaten
3 tbsp	milk
1 tbsp	vanilla
2 ¼ cups	all-purpose flour
⅔ cup	cocoa powder
1 tsp	baking soda
1 tsp	salt
1 ½ cups	chopped nuts such as pecans or walnuts
1 cup	chocolate chips

1. Preheat oven to 350F. Lightly grease one or two cookie sheets. Beat butter in a large bowl until creamy. Gradually beat in granulated and brown sugars until light and fluffy. Then beat in eggs, one at a time, and the milk and vanilla until well blended.

2. Sift flour with cocoa, baking soda and salt in a medium-sized bowl. Gradually add the flour mixture to the butter mixture until well blended. Stir in nuts and chocolate chips.

3. Drop by heaping tablespoon about 3 inches apart on the prepared cookie sheets. Bake for 10 to 13 minutes. Remove and cool on a rack. Cookies will keep well in an airtight container for several days. They also freeze well.

Per cookie: 129 calories, 1.4 g protein, 8.4 g fat, 13.3 g carbohydrates, 1 g dietary fibre, 10 mg calcium, 0.6 mg iron

DEBBIE'S WHIPPED SHORTBREAD

MW READER RECIPE: Holiday baking would not be complete without a shortbread recipe. Here's an easy recipe for novice shortbread bakers from Debra Laval of Calgary. After watching her friend Debbie make these cookies, Debra pried the recipe from her and found it "so simple it was ridiculous!"

Makes 4 ½ to 5 dozen

1 lb	butter, preferably unsalted
1 cup	icing sugar
3 cups	all-purpose flour
	Decorations: red or green candied cherry halves,
	M&M candies, chocolate chips, Smarties, almonds
	or pecans

1.   Preheat oven to 350F. In the large bowl of an electric mixer, beat butter with icing sugar until light. Gradually add flour and beat until they are combined. Do not overbeat or cookies will be too crumbly.

2.   Drop by small tablespoonfuls onto ungreased cookie sheets, spacing them about 2 inches apart. Place your favourite decoration in the centre of each cookie. Bake for 10 to 14 minutes, until cookies are light golden on the bottom but still fairly white on top. Let them cool on cookie sheet for 5 minutes, then transfer to racks to cool completely.

Per cookie: 84 calories, 0.7 g protein, 6.2 g fat, 6.5 g carbohydrates, 0.2 g dietary fibre, 3 mg calcium, 0.3 mg iron

TIPS

If you are sending cookie gifts across the country, make sure you choose ones that are fairly firm. Pack the cookies in a cookie tin or other sturdy container. Fill it about three-quarters full, then top with a piece of bubble wrap before putting on the lid. Wrap the container in bubble wrap, then put it in a box. Mark "Fragile" on the outside of the box, mail — and cross your fingers.

SUPER PEANUT BUTTER OATMEAL COOKIES

MW READER RECIPE: It's always tough to choose a favourite recipe from our Great Canadian Cookie swap collection, but this one was a sure winner. It comes from Nancy Bradshaw and she says the recipe can be easily cut in half.

Makes 7 dozen

3 ½ cups	flour (unbleached or white all-purpose, whole wheat, or a combination)
2 tsp	baking soda
1 tsp	salt
1 cup	butter or margarine, at room temperature
1 cup	chunky peanut butter, at room temperature
2 cups	granulated sugar
2 cups	brown sugar
4	eggs
2 tsp	vanilla
4 cups	rolled oats
⅔ cup each	chocolate chips, raisins, walnuts and coconut

1.   Preheat oven to 350F. Lightly grease several cookie sheets. Stir flour with baking soda and salt in a medium-sized bowl. Set aside.

2.   Beat butter with peanut butter in a large bowl until smooth and creamy. Beat in sugars until well blended. Beat in eggs, one at a time, beating after each addition. Beat in vanilla. Gradually beat in the flour mixture until well blended. Then stir in oats, chocolate chips, raisins, walnuts and coconut.

3.   Drop by tablespoonfuls, about 2 inches apart, on prepared cookie sheets. Bake for 12 to 14 minutes or until bottoms and tops of cookies are golden. Time will vary depending on size of spoonful. Remove to a rack to cool.

Per cookie: 133 calories, 2.5 g protein, 5.6 g fat, 19.4 g carbohydrates, 1 g dietary fibre, 13 mg calcium, 0.7 mg iron

Cookies frozen in airtight containers will keep well for up to a month. An alternative is to freeze the cookie dough (wrap it well in plastic wrap, then in foil) until you have time to bake them. When you're ready to use the dough, thaw it in the refrigerator.

PARKINS

MW READER RECIPE: This old-fashioned recipe from Mary Martin of Surrey, B.C., was originally her mother's. Everyone in Mary's family loves them, including her six grandchildren.

Makes 6 ½ dozen

3 cups	all-purpose flour
2 ½ cups	rolled oats
2 cups	granulated sugar
4 tsp	baking soda
1 tsp	cinnamon
1 tsp	ground ginger
1 tsp	allspice
1 tsp	salt
⅔ cup	all-vegetable shortening
½ cup	margarine or butter
2	eggs, lightly beaten
½ cup	warm corn syrup

1.   Preheat oven to 350F. In a large bowl, combine flour, oats, sugar, baking soda, spices and salt until well blended. Using your fingers, rub in shortening and margarine until thoroughly mixed. Add eggs and warm syrup and mix well. (It is very important that the syrup be warm or the dough will not hold together.)
2.   Roll into 1-inch balls and place them on parchment-lined cookie sheets. Bake for 8 to 12 minutes, or until a deep golden brown. Watch carefully to prevent burning. Cool on a rack. Cookies will firm as they cool.

Per cookie: 81 calories, 1.1 g protein, 3.2 g fat, 12.1 g carbohydrates, 0.5 g dietary fibre, 5 mg calcium, 0.4 mg iron, 2 mcg folacin

AMAZING OATMEAL COOKIES

MW READER RECIPE: Carla Andor of Oshawa, Ontario, found this recipe among her grandmother's things. "I'd been searching for years for an amazing oatmeal cookie and I believe this is it," she says. "I think the secret to their great taste is the almond extract."

Makes about 4 ½ dozen

1 cup	margarine or butter
1 cup	granulated sugar
1 cup	brown sugar
2	eggs
1 tsp	almond extract
2 cups	all-purpose flour
1 tsp	baking soda
1 tsp	salt
2 cups	rolled oats

1. Preheat oven to 350F. Grease several cookie sheets. Using an electric mixer, beat margarine with sugars until blended. Beat in eggs and almond extract until combined.

2. Beat in flour, baking soda and salt until combined. Stir in rolled oats. Drop by tablespoonfuls onto a greased cookie sheet, then flatten with a floured fork. Bake for 10 to 15 minutes, or until a deep golden brown. Transfer cookies to a rack to cool.

Per cookie: 102 calories, 1.4 g protein, 4.2 g fat, 14.9 g carbohydrates, 0.6 g dietary fibre, 9 mg calcium, 0.5 mg iron, 2 mcg folacin

TIPS Why not freeze half the dough to bake another time?

COCONUT CHEWS

one POT *MW* READER RECIPE: Ann Scott of Calgary gave us her recipe for the tastiest, easiest squares ever. You can make them ahead and freeze them — and best of all, you need only one pot, so cleanup is easy.

Makes 36

¼ cup	butter
1 cup	brown sugar
1	egg

1 tsp	vanilla
½ cup	all-purpose flour
1 tsp	baking powder
½ tsp	salt
¾ cup	sweetened shredded coconut

1.   Preheat oven to 350F. Grease and flour an 8-inch square baking pan. Melt butter in a medium saucepan. Stir in brown sugar until dissolved. Remove from heat and cool slightly.
2.   Beat in egg and vanilla. In a separate bowl, sift together flour, baking powder and salt. Add the flour mixture to the sugar mixture and combine well. Stir in coconut.
3.   Spread the mixture in the pan and bake for 20 minutes or until a deep golden color. Cool in the pan on a rack. Cut into squares while slightly warm.

Per portion: 76 calories, 0.6 g protein, 3 g fat, 11.8 g carbohydrates, 0.3 g dietary fibre, 15 mg calcium, 0.4 mg iron, 1 mcg folacin

MONKEY CAKE

MW READER RECIPE: Elizabeth Starret of Orangeville, Ontario, sent us her recipe for this oatmeal bar: the very first thing she ever baked. She still loves it, especially now that she can bake it with her children (who insist on bigger portions).

Makes 25

½ cup	butter
½ cup	brown sugar
2 cups	rolled oats
1 tsp	vanilla

1.   Preheat oven to 350F. Grease an 8-inch square baking pan. Melt butter in a small saucepan over low heat. Remove from heat and stir in sugar, oats and vanilla until well mixed. Press into prepared pan.
2.   Bake for 15 to 20 minutes, watching carefully, until it is a deep golden brown. Cool on a rack, then refrigerate to cool completely before cutting into bars or squares.

Per portion: 74 calories, 1.1 g protein, 4.1 g fat, 8.6 g carbohydrates, 0.7 g dietary fibre, 8 mg calcium, 0.4 mg iron, 2 mcg folacin

PINEAPPLE SQUARES

MW READER RECIPE: Kim Hancocks of Agincourt, Ontario, gave us her recipe for these easy-as-can-be squares. Her mother found the recipe over 30 years ago in a cookbook compiled to raise money for a small Windsor hospital.

Makes 25

Crust

¾ cup	butter, at room temperature
¼ cup	granulated sugar
1 ½ cups	all-purpose flour
¼ tsp	salt

Topping

1	14-oz can crushed pineapple
1	egg
¾ cup	brown sugar
½ cup	sweetened shredded coconut
½ tsp	vanilla
¼ tsp	salt

1. Preheat oven to 350F. To make the crust, use an electric mixer to beat butter with sugar until well blended. Stir in flour and salt until combined. Press the crust mixture into an ungreased 8-inch square baking pan.

2. To make the topping, thoroughly drain pineapple by placing it in a sieve and pressing firmly with the back of a spoon to remove all the liquid. Scatter pineapple over the crust. In a medium-sized bowl, beat the egg and brown sugar, coconut, vanilla and salt. Gently spread the mixture over pineapple, keeping pineapple in place as much as possible. Bake for about 35 minutes, or until topping is a deep golden brown. Cool completely on a rack before cutting into squares.

Per portion: 128 calories, 1.2 g protein, 6.5 g fat, 16.8 g carbohydrates, 0.5 g dietary fibre, 11 mg calcium, 0.6 mg iron, 3 mcg folacin

BONANZAS

MW READER RECIPE: Daniela Karageorgos of Toronto started making these light and delectable cookies in her junior high home economics class. They're always eaten as fast as she makes them.

Makes about 2 ½ dozen

2 cups	all-purpose flour
1 tbsp	granulated sugar
3 ½ tsp	baking powder
½ tsp	salt
5 tbsp	all-vegetable shortening
¾ cup	milk
⅓ cup	apple or raspberry jelly (approximately)

1.   Preheat oven to 350F. Lightly grease several cookie sheets. In a medium-sized bowl, combine flour, sugar, baking powder and salt. Cut in shortening until it is fully incorporated into flour and fine crumbs form. Stir in as much milk as needed to form a soft dough. Gather the mixture into a ball; knead about five times on a lightly floured surface.

2.   On a lightly floured surface, roll the dough into a square shape about ⅛ inch thick. Cut the dough into 2 ½-inch squares. Place about 1 teaspoon jelly in the centre of a square. Bring the four corners of the square to the centre and pinch them together firmly. Pinch the sides to seal closed. (The dough must be pinched together firmly or the jelly will leak during baking.) Scraps of dough can be rerolled.

3.   Place the cookies on the prepared baking sheets. Bake for 15 to 20 minutes or until golden brown. Cool on a rack.

Per cookie: 63 calories, 1.1 g protein, 2.3 g fat, 9.6 g carbohydrates, 0.3 g dietary fibre, 23 mg calcium, 0.4 mg iron, 2 mcg folacin

AUNT LILA'S DROP COOKIES

MW READER RECIPE: Evelyn Tackaberry of Ottawa has been making these cookies for 65 years. Light in texture, they're also pretty on a platter.

Makes about 2 ½ dozen

1 cup	all-purpose flour
1 cup	cornstarch
½ cup	granulated sugar
2 tsp	baking powder
	Pinch of salt
¾ cup	cold butter or margarine, cut into ½-inch pieces
1	egg, lightly beaten
½ cup	seedless raspberry or apricot jelly (approximately)

1.   Preheat oven to 350F. Lightly grease several cookie sheets. In a large bowl, combine flour, cornstarch, sugar, baking powder and salt. Cut butter into the dry ingredients until it is completely incorporated and crumbs form.
2.   Gradually add just enough beaten egg to the flour mixture so that the dough can be gathered into a ball. If necessary, add a bit more egg or water. (The dough should not be sticky.)
3.   With your fingers floured, form the dough into 1-inch balls and place them on the prepared cookie sheets. Flour your thumb and make a small dent in the centre of each. Fill the dent with about ½ teaspoon jelly. Bake for 20 to 25 minutes, or until golden.

Per cookie: 104 calories, 0.9 g protein, 5 g fat, 14 g carbohydrates, 0.2 g dietary fibre, 12 mg calcium, 0.3 mg iron, 2 mcg folacin

OLD-FASHIONED GINGERSNAPS

MW READER RECIPE: These gingersnaps are the favourite recipe of Peggy Mowry, whose Darwell, Alberta, cookie exchange inspired the annual feature in *MW*. Peggy says these are real keepers. Stored in an airtight container, they'll last forever.

Makes 4 dozen

3 cups	all-purpose flour
2 tsp	baking soda
1 tsp	ground ginger
1 tsp	cinnamon
½ tsp	salt
½ tsp	ground cloves
¾ cup	margarine or shortening
1 cup	well-packed brown sugar
1	egg
¾ cup	cooking molasses
1 cup	granulated sugar (for rolling cookies)

1. In a medium-sized bowl, sift flour with baking soda, ginger, cinnamon, salt and cloves.
2. Beat margarine in a large bowl until creamy. Gradually add the brown sugar, then beat in egg and molasses until well blended. Stir the flour mixture into the margarine mixture. Wrap dough in plastic wrap or waxed paper and refrigerate until firm enough to handle — about 1 hour.
3. Preheat oven to 350F. Shape the dough into 1 ½-inch balls and roll them in granulated sugar. Place the balls 2 inches apart on ungreased cookie sheets. Bake in preheated oven for 8 to 10 minutes. Watch carefully, as cookies burn easily. Cool on wire racks.

Per cookie: 101 calories, 1 g protein, 3 g fat, 17.9 g carbohydrates, 0.3 g dietary fibre, 16 mg calcium, 0.7 mg iron

SPICE BARS

MW READER RECIPE: Peggy Kontak of Halifax gave us her favourite not-too-sweet bar recipe that her mother used to make when Peggy was growing up.

Makes about 3 dozen

¾ cup	all-purpose flour
½ tsp	baking soda
½ tsp	nutmeg
½ tsp	cinnamon
½ tsp	salt
¼ tsp	ground cloves
½ cup	firmly packed brown sugar
1 cup	chopped nuts
1 cup	raisins
½ cup	vegetable oil
2	eggs, lightly beaten
1 tsp	vanilla
	Icing sugar for dusting

1. Preheat oven to 375F. Lightly grease a 9-inch square pan. Sift flour, baking soda, nutmeg, cinnamon, salt and cloves into a large bowl. Stir in brown sugar, nuts and raisins. In a separate bowl, whisk together oil, eggs and vanilla. Make a well in the centre of the dry ingredients and pour the oil mixture into the well, then stir until blended.
2. Pour the mixture into the prepared pan. Bake for 20 to 25 minutes until a cake tester inserted in the centre of the bars comes out clean. Cool in the pan on a rack. Dust with icing sugar.

Per bar: 89 calories, 1.3 g protein, 5.5 g fat, 9.4 g carbohydrates, 0.4 g dietary fibre, 11 mg calcium, 0.4 mg iron

OLE'S OATMEAL SUPERCOOKIES

MW READER RECIPE: This recipe from Genevieve Heskar of Burnaby, B.C., calls for just about everything-but-the-kitchen-sink, and it's a great crowd pleaser.

Makes 5 dozen

1 cup	all-purpose flour
¼ cup	oat bran (optional)
¾ tsp	salt
¾ tsp	baking soda
¾ tsp	baking powder
2 tsp	cinnamon
1 cup	shortening
½ cup	peanut butter
2 cups	granulated sugar
3	eggs
¼ cup	milk
2 tsp	vanilla
1 cup	chocolate chips
½ cup	nuts
½ cup	raisins
3 ½ cups	rolled oats

1. Preheat oven to 350F. Line two cookie sheets with foil and set aside. In a medium-sized bowl, stir together flour, oat bran, salt, baking soda, baking powder and cinnamon; set aside. In a large bowl, beat shortening with peanut butter until fluffy. Beat in sugar, then eggs, milk and vanilla until well blended. Beat in the flour mixture until well mixed.
2. Stir in chocolate chips, nuts, raisins and oats. It may be necessary to knead the dough with your hands to make sure everything is well mixed. Drop by the tablespoon on the foil-lined baking sheets a couple of inches apart. Bake for 12 to 15 minutes a side, switching cookie sheets in the oven during the last 5 minutes. Leave the cookies on the sheets to cool for 2 minutes, then transfer them to racks to cool completely. Wipe the foil and use it again.

Per cookie: 124 calories, 2.2 g protein, 6.6 g fat, 14.9 g carbohydrates, 1 g dietary fibre, 11 mg calcium, 0.5 mg iron

If you're making these cookies for a big cookie exchange, you can double the recipe.

BUTTER TART SQUARES

MW READER RECIPE: Marnie Franks of Ottawa says these squares are a real time-saver if you need a dessert in a hurry. She calls them "an old-fashioned favourite for modern times."

Makes 16 squares

Base

½ cup	butter or margarine, at room temperature
1 cup	all-purpose flour
2 tbsp	granulated sugar

Filling

1 ½ cups	brown sugar
1 cup	chopped walnuts
½ cup	raisins
3	eggs
3 tbsp	all-purpose flour
½ tsp	baking powder
1 tsp	vanilla

1.   Preheat oven to 350F. Beat butter with flour and sugar until well blended. Press the mixture firmly into an ungreased 9-inch square pan. Bake for 15 minutes.
2.   Meanwhile, stir together all the filling ingredients. Remove the base from the oven and gently spread the filling ingredients over the hot base. Return to the oven and continue to bake for 20 to 25 minutes until the filling is a deep golden brown. Filling may be slightly jiggly in the centre, but will firm upon cooling.
3.   Cool completely and cut into squares or bars.

Per square: 249 calories, 3.5 g protein, 11.7 g fat, 34.3 g carbohydrates, 1 g dietary fibre, 39 mg calcium, 1.3 mg iron

These squares can be made in advance, then frozen. Stored in an airtight container, the squares will keep for several months. Once thawed, all cookies and squares should be stored in an airtight container in the fridge or at room temperature.

CHOCOLATE AND PEANUT BUTTER CHIP COOKIES

MW READER RECIPE: These easy-to-make cookies are an old standby of Margot Forsyth of Toronto from late-night study sessions in her university days.

Makes 4 dozen

1 ½ cups	all-purpose flour
1 tsp	baking soda
1 tsp	salt
1 cup	butter, at room temperature
¾ cup	brown sugar
¾ cup	granulated sugar
2	eggs, lightly beaten
1 tsp	vanilla
1	300-g pkg chocolate or peanut butter chips
1 cup	chopped nuts or raisins
2 cups	rolled oats

1. Preheat oven to 350F. Lightly grease several cookie sheets. In a large bowl, stir together flour, baking soda and salt. In a separate bowl, beat the butter with the brown sugar and granulated sugar until well mixed. Beat in eggs and vanilla. Beat the flour mixture into the butter mixture until combined. Stir in chocolate chips, nuts and rolled oats.

2. Drop by tablespoon onto cookie sheets and flatten slightly with a fork. Bake for 10 to 12 minutes. Remove from oven and transfer to a rack to cool.

Per cookie: 138 calories, 1.9 g protein, 8.1 g fat, 15.7 g carbohydrates, 1.1 g dietary fibre, 12 mg calcium, 0.7 mg iron

 If you store several kinds of cookies or squares together in one container, the texture of each may change — for example, crisp cookies may become chewier — and flavors may blend together. Storing cookies that contain peanut butter with other cookies may make the other cookies taste slightly of peanut butter. Be very careful of peanut allergies!

BUTTERMILK BROWNIES

*MW*READER RECIPE: Carol Boulanger of Fort McMurray, Alberta, submitted this delicious, moist brownie recipe. The buttermilk makes it irresistible, but Carol has occasionally substituted 1% milk and they turn out just as well.

Makes about 36 brownies

Brownies

2 cups	all-purpose flour
2 cups	granulated sugar
1 tsp	baking soda
¼ tsp	salt
1 cup	butter or margarine
⅓ cup	cocoa powder
1 cup	water
2	eggs
½ cup	buttermilk
1 ½ tsp	vanilla

Icing

¼ cup	butter or margarine
3 tbsp	unsweetened cocoa
3 tbsp	buttermilk
2 ¼ cups	icing sugar
½ tsp	vanilla
¾ cup	chopped pecans

1.   To make brownies: Preheat oven to 350F. Lightly butter a 13 x 9-inch baking pan. In a large bowl, combine flour, sugar, baking soda and salt. In a small saucepan, bring butter, cocoa powder and water to a boil, stirring continuously. Remove from heat. Beat the butter and cocoa mixture into the flour mixture until well combined. Add eggs, buttermilk and vanilla; beat for 1 minute.
2.   Pour into the prepared pan and bake for 25 minutes, or until a toothpick inserted in the centre comes out clean. Cool in the pan on a rack for about 15 minutes.

3. To make icing: While the brownies are cooling, heat butter, cocoa and buttermilk in a small saucepan, stirring continuously until butter is melted and the mixture is very warm. Remove from heat and beat in icing sugar and vanilla until smooth. Stir in pecans. Gently spread the icing over the warm brownies.

> *Per brownie: 176 calories, 1.7 g protein, 8.7 g fat, 24.2 g carbohydrates,*
> *0.8 g dietary fibre, 13 mg calcium, 0.5 mg iron*

HAZELNUT MACAROONS

MW READER RECIPE: Talin Hacat of Don Mills, Ontario, sent us this recipe for Hazelnut Macaroons. These three-ingredient cookies are perfect when you feel like having something sweet and not too heavy.

Makes about 3 ½ dozen

3	egg whites, at room temperature
¾ cup	granulated sugar
2 cups	very finely ground hazelnuts

1. Preheat oven to 350F. Lightly grease a few cookie sheets, line them with waxed paper, then lightly grease them again. Using an electric mixer on high speed, beat egg whites until frothy. Gradually add sugar, 1 tablespoon at a time. Continue to beat egg whites until stiff peaks form. Fold in nuts.
2. Place generous teaspoons of the mixture, spaced 1 ½ inches apart, on the cookie sheets. Bake for 13 to 15 minutes, or until lightly browned.

> *Per cookie: 42 calories, 0.7 g protein, 2.2 g fat, 5.3 g carbohydrates,*
> *0.2 g dietary fibre, 7 mg calcium, 0.1 mg iron*

When making our hazelnut macaroons, or beating egg whites for other cookies or cakes, keep these pointers in mind: beat egg whites in a very clean bowl that has no traces of oil. Avoid beating whites in plastic bowls, as it is difficult to remove all traces of oil from them. Adding a pinch of salt or cream of tartar to whites helps stabilize them.

LENORE'S ALMOND SQUARES

MW READER RECIPE: These delicious can't-get-enough almond squares were sent to us by Shirley Pomerleau of Morinville, Alberta. She was given the recipe at a cookie exchange in 1989. Since then, it has become one of Shirley's favourites.

Makes 25 squares

Base

1 ¼ cups	all-purpose flour
½ cup	butter, at room temperature
2 tbsp	icing sugar

Topping

4 tbsp	butter
1 cup	brown sugar
¼ cup	half-and-half (10% cream)
1 tsp	vanilla
1 cup	sliced almonds

1. To prepare base: Preheat oven to 350F. Lightly grease a 9-inch square baking pan. Using your hands, blend flour with butter and icing sugar in a medium bowl until well mixed. Pat evenly into pan. Bake for 10 minutes.
2. To prepare topping: Combine butter, brown sugar, cream and vanilla in a small saucepan and bring to a boil. Boil for 3 minutes, then remove from heat and stir in almonds. Spread the almond mixture evenly on the cooked base. Bake for another 10 to 13 minutes.
3. Remove from oven. The filling will still be bubbling and will set upon cooling. After the filling has cooled completely, cut into squares.

Per square: 128 calories, 1.4 g protein, 7.4 g fat, 14.5 g carbohydrates, 0.4 g dietary fibre, 20 mg calcium, 0.6 mg iron

TIPS MW

Buy nuts in stores where the turnover is high; nuts can go rancid quickly and they'll spoil your baking efforts. Leftover nuts are best stored well wrapped in the refrigerator or freezer.

CHEWY CHOCOLATE CHOCOLATE CHIP COOKIES

MW READER RECIPE: "As a self-confessed cookie addict, I'm always making variations of my favourite recipes," writes Cheryl Tien of Oakville, Ontario. "This is one I hope will be passed down through generations. Every time I bring a batch to the office, someone asks for the recipe."

Makes 3 ½ dozen

1 cup	butter or margarine, at room temperature
1 ⅔ cup	granulated sugar
2	eggs
2 tsp	vanilla
2 cups	all-purpose flour
¾ cup	cocoa, sifted
1 tsp	baking soda
1 cup	chocolate chips (semisweet, white or a combination)
½ cup	chopped macademia nuts or pecans (optional)

1. Preheat oven to 350F. Using an electric mixer, beat butter and sugar until light and fluffy. Add eggs and vanilla and beat on low until blended. In a separate bowl, combine the dry ingredients until well blended, then beat them into the butter mixture. Stir in chocolate chips and nuts, if using.

2. Drop by heaping teaspoon, about 2 inches apart, onto ungreased baking sheets. Bake for about 8 minutes. Remove from oven; let stand for 1 to 2 minutes on the cookie sheets before removing the cookies to a rack to cool.

Per cookie: 120 calories, 1.4 g protein, 6.5 g fat, 15.5 g carbohydrates, 1 g dietary fibre, 7 mg calcium, 0.6 mg iron

When you're baking, it is very important to read the entire recipe before you begin. Make sure to preheat the oven, grease the pans if necessary, and assemble all ingredients before starting.

THE ULTIMATE NANAIMO BAR

Who better to give us this recipe than the Nanaimo Chamber of Commerce? According to local legend, a woman from Nanaimo, B.C., entered her recipe for chocolate squares, which she had proudly named after her hometown, in a magazine recipe contest. A second legend prevails in Nanaimo that around the turn of the century, many of the young coal miners who came from Britain brought these squares, which their mothers had packed to sustain them during their long journey to Canada.

Makes 20 squares

Bottom Layer

½ cup	unsalted butter
¼ cup	granulated sugar
5 tbsp	unsweetened cocoa powder
1	egg, lightly beaten
1 ¾ cups	graham wafer crumbs
1 cup	shredded coconut
½ cup	finely chopped almonds

Second Layer

½ cup	unsalted butter
3 tbsp	table cream or milk
2 tbsp	custard powder
2 cups	sifted icing sugar

Third Layer

4 oz	semisweet chocolate, chopped
2 tbsp	unsalted butter

1. Bottom Layer: Melt butter with sugar and cocoa in the top of a double boiler over simmering water. Add egg and stir continuously just until thickened, about 5 minutes. Remove from heat; stir in graham wafer crumbs, coconut and almonds. Press firmly into a lightly greased 8-inch square pan.
2. Second Layer: Beat butter with cream, custard powder and icing sugar until well combined and light and creamy. Spread over the bottom layer. Refrigerate.

3.   Third Layer: Melt chocolate with butter over low heat until melted. Cool, so that chocolate is still liquid but not hot. Pour evenly over second layer. Refrigerate squares before cutting.

Per square: 263 calories, 2.5 g protein, 17.6 g fat, 27.4 g carbohydrates, 1.5 g dietary fibre, 22 mg calcium, 0.9 mg iron

CRISP AND CHEWIES

MW READER RECIPE: Evelyn Gilbert and her daughter Jan run the Edmonton Creative Crafts Store in Edmonton. Although they teach the skilled art of cake decorating, when they're looking for a tasty, easy recipe to make for home, here's what they bake.

Makes about 3 dozen

¾ cup	butter, at room temperature
1 cup	granulated or brown sugar
¼ cup	light molasses (fancy, not cooking)
1	egg
1 ½ cups	all-purpose flour
1 tsp	baking soda
1 tsp	salt
½ tsp	ground cloves
½ tsp	ground ginger
1 ¾ cups	rolled oats

1.   Preheat oven to 350F. Beat butter with sugar until light and fluffy. Beat in molasses and egg until well combined. In a separate bowl, stir together flour, baking soda, salt and spices until blended.
2.   Beat the flour mixture into the butter mixture until combined. Stir in oats. Drop by the spoonful onto ungreased baking sheets (cookies spread, so space them at least 3 inches apart). Bake for 8 to 10 minutes or until a deep brown color. Do not overbake, or the cookies will not be chewy. If you have difficulty removing the cookies from the baking sheet, let them stand for about 1 minute before removing. Cool on a rack.

Per cookie: 89 calories, 1 g protein, 4.1 g fat, 12.1 g carbohydrates, 0.4 g dietary fibre, 8 mg calcium, 0.4 mg iron

GRANDAD TOM'S CUCKOOS

MW READER RECIPE: Liz Yedlinski, of Edmonton, Alberta, remembers that Grandad Tom's Cuckoos were her great-grandfather's favourite cookies. They freeze well and the recipe doubles or triples easily.

Makes 2 ½ dozen

½ cup	butter or margarine
½ cup	granulated sugar
½ cup	packed brown sugar
1	egg
1 tsp	vanilla
1 cup	all-purpose flour
½ tsp	baking soda
½ tsp	salt
½ cup each	chocolate and butterscotch chips
½ cup	chopped walnuts or pecan pieces

1. Preheat oven to 350F. Lightly grease one or two cookie sheets. Beat butter with granulated and brown sugar in a large bowl until light and fluffy. Beat in egg and vanilla until well combined. Stir together flour, baking soda and salt in a small bowl. Beat the flour mixture into the butter mixture. Stir in chocolate and butterscotch chips and walnuts.
2. Drop by tablespoon, placing each about 2 inches apart on prepared cookie sheets. Bake for 10 to 12 minutes. Remove the cookies from the cookie sheet and cool them on a rack. Stored in an airtight container, cookies keep well for several days.

Per cookie: 108 calories, 1.3 g protein, 6.4 g fat, 12 g carbohydrates, 4.0 g dietary fibre, 7 mg calcium, 0.4 mg iron

For a variation, Liz suggests stirring in 1/2 to 1 cup oatmeal with the chips and nuts.

RAISIN SQUARES

MW READER RECIPE: Whenever Ida Clodman of North York, Ontario, has a dinner party, her friends request her raisin squares.

Makes 36

Filling

1 ⅓ cups	raisins
¾ cup	granulated sugar
2 tbsp	all-purpose flour
1 cup	boiling water
½ tsp	orange juice or vanilla
	Pinch of salt

Base and Topping

2 cups	all-purpose flour
1 cup	granulated sugar
1 tsp	baking powder
1 cup	butter or margarine
1	egg, lightly beaten

1. Preheat oven to 350F. Lightly grease a 9-inch square baking pan. Make the filling by stirring raisins, sugar and flour together in a saucepan. Add water and bring to a boil, then reduce heat and simmer uncovered, stirring frequently, until thick — 5 to 8 minutes. Remove from heat and stir in orange juice and salt.
2. To make the base and topping: In a large bowl, blend flour, sugar and baking powder. Cut in butter, using your fingertips or a pastry cutter, until small crumbs form. Stir in egg until blended. Gather the dough into a ball. Flour your fingers and pat half the mixture into the prepared pan. Gently spread the raisin filling over the top. Pat together the remaining pastry in a thin sheet and piece it together over the raisin filling. (If there are a few small holes in the topping they will disappear during baking.)
3. Bake for 25 to 35 minutes, or until slightly golden brown. Cool on a rack.

Per portion: 128 calories, 1.2 g protein, 6.5 g fat, 16.8 g carbohydrates, 0.5 g dietary fibre, 11 mg calcium, 0.6 mg iron, 3 mcg folacin

CREAMY CARAMEL FUDGE

MW READER RECIPE: Cynthia Richard of Montreal, Quebec, gave us this recipe for Creamy Caramel Fudge. Instead of making fudge with costly maple syrup, she uses brown sugar. The results are incredibly smooth and delicious, and the price is right!

Makes 25

3 cups	light brown sugar
1 cup	granulated sugar
2 tbsp	all-purpose flour
2 tsp	baking powder
1 cup	milk
1 cup	whipping cream
1 tbsp	butter
1 tsp	vanilla
	Pinch of salt

1.   Butter an 8-inch square baking pan. In a large deep saucepan, stir together brown sugar, granulated sugar, flour and baking powder. Stir in milk and whipping cream until blended.

2.   Over medium-high heat, stirring just until sugar dissolves, bring to a boil. The mixture will foam vigorously. Boil, uncovered, without stirring, until the mixture reaches a soft ball stage (239F on a candy thermometer)—10 to 15 minutes. Remove from heat; do not stir. Let stand until the mixture is warm to the touch. Don't worry if there is a bit of foam on the surface.

3.   Using a wooden spoon, stir in butter, vanilla and salt. Continue to stir with the wooden spoon just until mixture loses its sheen and turns lighter in color— 2 to 3 minutes. Immediately pour it into the pan, spreading to fill the pan. Cut into squares while fudge is still warm. Fudge will keep well in an airtight container for several days.

Per square: 172 calories, 0.6 g protein, 4 g fat, 34.7 g carbohydrates, 0.2 g dietary fibre, 50 mg calcium, 0.6 mg iron

INDEX

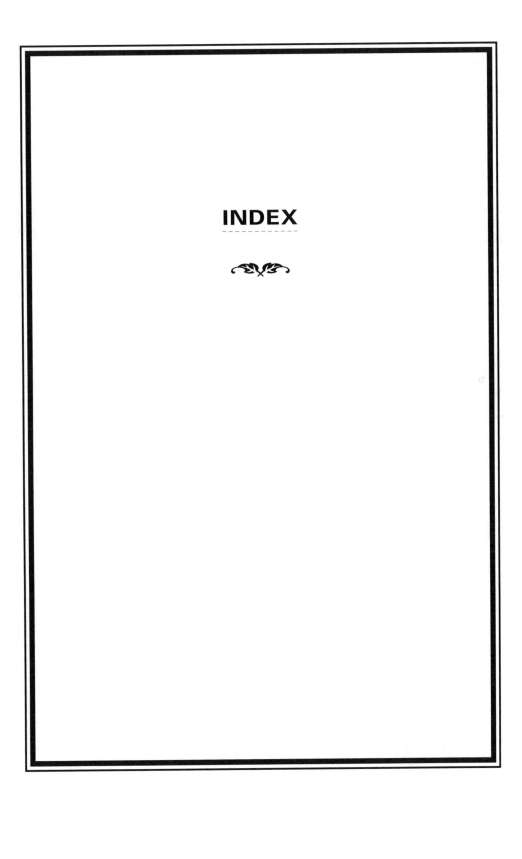